Paloma

Tell me.....

WHAT'S YOUR POINT?

THE BRAND ARROW

DEFINE YOUR POINT. GROW YOUR BRAND

BRUCE M MCKINNON

Copyright © 2019 Bruce M McKinnon

22 21 20 19   7 6 5 4 3 2 1

First published 2019 by Malcolm Down and Sarah Grace Publishing
www.malcolmdown.co.uk

The right of Bruce M McKinnon to be identified as the author of this work has
been asserted by him in accordance with the Copyright,
Designs and Patents Act 1988.

British Library Cataloguing in Publication Data
A catalogue record for this book is available from the British Library.

ISBN 978-1-912863-23-5

Cover design by Sally Davidson
Art direction by Sarah Grace

To Naomi and Ron

CONTENTS

FOREWORD

It is an honor for me to share my experience with Bruce McKinnon over the past 24 years.

In 1995, as CEO, I hired Bruce to create a new name and identity for Self Help Crafts, an importer and seller of handcrafted gifts based in the US. Bruce pushed us hard ("What's your point?!") to sort out who we were and what our mission goal was. The result was a brand strategy that delivered the name Ten Thousand Villages, and a powerful new logo. Sales grew dramatically over the next 15 years. It was one of the two most significant things I did as CEO over 17 years.

Bruce works easily with people, with a clear focus on getting the truth without fuzzy flim-flam. It is critical to Bruce that he takes everyone with him in the process. He takes the time to accomplish it. His communication style is comfortable and effective. Excellent market tested results are essential to him. He is equally effective in a corporate boardroom, a church hall or a coffee shop.

Bruce also happens to be a Christian who is humble and yet works hard to integrate his faith in all he does. It is a special gift to those with whom he works. If you are a sole trader, a start-up, consultant, small or large business, read this book and if possible call on Bruce himself. I recommend him fully. He is warm, passionate and inspirational in all he does.

Paul Myers

CEO, Ten Thousand Villages (1989 - 2006), Chairman, World Fair Trade Organization (1993-1999, 2007-2011)

INTRODUCTION
The Role of This Book and How to Use It

"What's the name all about, Jeff?"

I was having coffee with the co-founder and president of Just Us! Coffee Cooperative in Nova Scotia and it seemed I had just asked a difficult question.

Names are tricky; quite often what seems like a great idea at the time is either forgotten or not seen as relevant anymore. But to be fair, it is an unusual name – and it had an exclamation mark – so I was curious as to how it came about.

"Well, let's see." Jeff took a sip of coffee and after a moment told me the name sounded a little like "justice" and as the co-op roasts and distributes fair trade coffee, it seemed appropriate.

"No," I said, "there has to be a better reason."

"Well it was 20 years ago," he replied, and went back to his coffee to muse some more on the question.

As he ruminated I thought back to the story of how it all started. Jeff Moore and his wife Debra, two social workers, along with three friends, were moved by the stories of the hardships endured by small-scale coffee growers and decided to do something about it.

Jeff flew down to Chiapas in Mexico and after a couple of days called Debra and they both agreed to buy an 18-tonne shipping container of coffee – once Debra had secured a second mortgage on their home to pay for it! And when it arrived – on their front lawn – there was the small matter of how to store, roast, pack, sell and ship the stuff.

Those pioneers went from Canada's first fair trade coffee roaster to running a hugely successful cooperative selling coffee, tea and chocolate to countless cafes and stores across the country as well as delivering significant benefits to the small farmers who they worked with.

Rightly or not, I felt a more compelling story behind the name needed to be rooted out.

"Ah yes – that's it," cried Jeff. "We're a small organization fighting against the big corporations for the rights of small farmers; there's 'just us' against the big guys."

"No, come on Jeff, is that really it?"

> *"The job of a brand strategy is to rediscover, capture or create a set of truths about an organization."*

He returned to his coffee, and after what seemed like an age he looked at me and smiled broadly. "Now I remember." And what he told me made the hairs on the back of my neck stand up – so much so that I wrote it down, word for word, and here it is:

> You know, Bruce, we are all on this journey of life together – locally and globally. We are all part of the same human family. And as we visit our partners throughout the world and share their struggles, successes, and dreams, this connection has continued to drive us. At work, in the community, in society, and globally we all want the same things for ourselves, our community, our kids and the world.
>
> So the most powerful of all reasons for the name and the most concrete is the idea that there is no them and us, just us!

And in that moment of clarity, the beginning of the brand strategy was born! Those few words delivered a crystal-clear insight to their higher purpose, their passion, and their uniqueness that had, over the busy and successful decades, been lost. So, the job of a brand strategy is to rediscover, capture or create a set of truths about an organization and then legislate that truth.

Legislate? Write it down, choosing a small number of words very carefully, so that those charged with growing the organization know what they have in their hands and so can put the brand into the hands of their customers.

As a result, the name stopped being a kind of slightly quirky add-on to the brand and instead became the center of it - rooted in their story as real and authentic as you could ever wish for. It released an energy and purpose that every department at Just Us! shared as we developed an understanding of their value and how to express that value in a way that was relevant to their customers and different from the competition.

The point of this book

This book has been written to equip readers to be able to succinctly define the point of their business and then apply that point across their whole organization. Over the last 30 years working with brands, no matter what sector, product, service or geographical region, I've met clients who share a similar problem to Jeff.

Namely, bringing to the surface or distilling features and benefits, different target markets and audiences into a unified purpose or point is tough. That to be able to express the offer in a single-minded way that can be universally applied is a challenge most find difficult to meet.

Not surprising as it's not easy! But it's a challenge worth pursuing because having a point means a business has more chance of sticking in the minds of customers and more chance of providing clear direction to the team charged with making the brand a success.

Points are useful as they're sharp, tend to stick into things and there's just one of them (think arrow). Being singular means a single focus - only one thing to communicate. The oft-told story still remains true, that it's easier to catch one tennis ball than twenty - just don't try the exercise with arrows.

It stands to reason that a company that is aligned behind a shared point will have a better chance of success than one that isn't. So the role of a brand strategy is to marshal every aspect of an organization into a single direction that will provide crystal-clear clarity for both the customer and the business itself. And to be successful, a brand strategy needs to engage every part of the business - not just the marketing department.

It often takes an external perspective to be able to see the wood from the trees; what's blindingly obvious from the outside is often seemingly invisible from the inside. Or it takes someone like me being quite rude with my incessant questions – sorry Jeff.

"To be successful, a brand strategy needs to engage every part of the business."

So in 2009, I developed a tool to help my clients be able more easily to define the point of their organizations. The tool was, in reality, a series of questions around expressing a client's services and the benefits it delivers; how the customers' needs are being met; their ambition, and the drivers and barriers to that ambition. I found the process of engaging with these questions made it easier for the clients to define the point of their organizations and I subsequently have used this process in over 50 client projects across North America and Europe for all kinds of organizations in all kinds of sectors.

The ambition for this book is to replace me and to provide that external yet informed point of view that will deliver that clarity – so you can see the wood and trees!

Who the book is written for

Written in non-technical language, it is hoped that anyone will be able to understand the powerful role a brand strategy can play in an organization.

I had in mind when writing the book that it would be most suited to small to medium size organizations that have an established business, who want to ensure their assets are being used to maximum effect and that their resources are being invested in the most efficient way possible. Although the book is aimed at businesses, it is entirely possible to apply the thinking to any organization that seeks to engage an audience – charities, churches, campaign organizations, etc.

The book is also for entrepreneurs and start-up businesses who are looking to "sense check" their ideas, and to make sure their offer is both relevant to their buyers and differentiated from what's already in the market. It can be used to inform their launch plans and demonstrate due diligence to potential investors.

Whilst the book is not aimed at CEOs of Fortune 500 companies or planning directors of multinational media agencies who have an abundance of resources to tackle this subject, the principles contained within the book have been rigorously developed in the world of commerce and would be equally useful to that audience.

Developing the brand strategy

Firstly, we will look at what brands are, why we value them and the role a brand strategy plays in first defining a vision and then marshaling an organization's resources to head toward that vision. A brand strategy should inform every part of the organization – what it produces, how it communicates, its culture, its customer and its brand (yes, the brand is a product of the brand strategy). We will then go on to define the four key elements that make up a brand strategy. These are:

1. Brand vision. Defining a vision, or destination, for the organization is critical because if the brand strategy is going to support and equip the organization to head toward it, then there must be clarity about where that is.

2. Brand positioning. This captures in one or two words how the brand is positioned in the minds of the people charged with creating and delivering it. The brand positioning is, in fact, the most important part of a brand because it is the root from which everything else grows.

3. Brand proposition. Often used as a tagline, the brand proposition expresses the brand's positioning to internal and external audiences. Its role is to be the start of the narrative of the brand, the first few words in the story about to be told.

4. Brand values. This describes how you should be able to sum up the character of an organization, how it behaves, the tone it uses in communications, how it presents itself to the world, how it treats its staff, and the products or services that it produces.

Applying the brand strategy

The book then goes to look at how a brand strategy can be used to meet an organization's challenges, like: What's our messaging and will it grow the business? How do we define our audiences and ensure they are the right ones? How can we make sure our marketing and sales activities are the best way of representing what we do? Specifically, it will cover:

- Brand name. Usually the first word in your story, it's also the most widely known, whether it's word of mouth or sitting on websites or business cards. So getting it right is fundamental to the success of your brand.

- The logo. Not the brand, rather a graphic representation of the brand strategy. A very important part of the presentation of the brand; after the name it will likely be its most widely known feature – so getting it right is essential.

- Audience. Broadly, there are three types of audience you will need to engage with. Those that deliver the brand – your team; those that consume the brand – your customers; and those that influence the brand – your stakeholders. All three have a role to play in making your brand a success.

- Messaging. This is using the brand strategy as a lens to look at how the brand can first identify the customer's problem and then provide a solution that is both relevant to their needs and different from the competition.

- Marketing. On its own, a brand strategy can do nothing. It needs to be applied, acted upon and communicated. That's the role of marketing – to marshal the insights from the brand strategy development process in order to engage and motivate an audience into action.

- Sales. Every organization needs to sell, whether it's ice cream or ideology, and the brand strategy has an important role to play in supporting the sales team. It should provide a hierarchy of features and benefits that will set the brand apart from the competition.

Throughout the book, I reference how some of the most successful companies in the world have used brand strategy, and at the conclusion of each chapter, I will share a case study from my own client experience.

The Brand Arrow – delivering the brand strategy

The final part of the book introduces the Brand Arrow framework. Based on the tools I have used in my own consulting business, it provides a logical structure to house and then apply the elements of the brand strategy. The arrow, as already stated, is a useful metaphor for delivering a point, and so the framework is based on the structure of an arrow.

So, for our Brand Arrow framework, the arrowhead represents the brand strategy; it defines the point of your brand and will stick in the minds of your customers.

The shaft contains the elements that will enable you to develop your key messaging which will direct how you present your brand in all your marketing and sales activity (website copy, sales pitches, brochures, etc.)

The feathers attached to the shaft ensure that the arrow stays on course. This is where the brand vision is housed; the destination that the whole organization is headed toward.

The target is the audience, the concentric circles signifying the relative importance of different customers – from primary to secondary and beyond. It also captures those that the brand wants to influence.

What the Brand Arrow looks like and what it's called are the logo and name respectively.

Each chapter finishes with two questions that are related to the content we have just gone through. The purpose of the questions is that by answering them, by the end of the book, you will have a pool of knowledge you can draw on to be able to complete and use the Brand Arrow.

This idea of a pool is one I use with my own clients: by the time the process has been worked through we will have all we need to go ahead and create a brand strategy. The only rule is that we only draw from that pool – this makes sure we use the work we have done together, as well as ensuring we don't allow random ideas to come into play. You'll see that each element of the Brand Arrow will reference which questions will provide the insights to complete it.

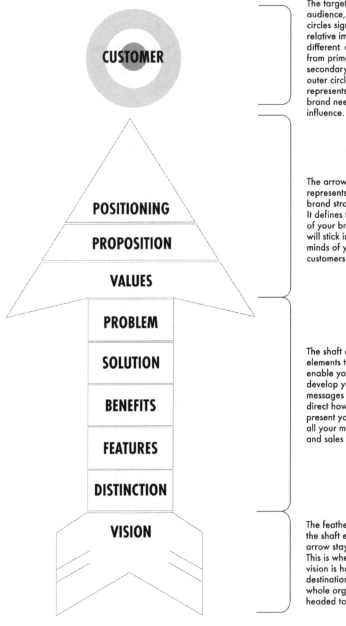

CUSTOMER

The target is the audience, the concentric circles signifying the relative importance of different customers – from primary to secondary and to the outer circle that represents those the brand needs to influence.

POSITIONING

PROPOSITION

VALUES

The arrow head represents the brand strategy. It defines the point of your brand and will stick in the minds of your customers.

PROBLEM

SOLUTION

BENEFITS

FEATURES

DISTINCTION

The shaft contains the elements that will enable you to develop your key messages which will direct how you present your brand in all your marketing and sales activity.

VISION

The feathers attached to the shaft ensure that the arrow stays on course. This is where the brand vision is housed, the destination that the whole organization is headed toward.

One important point: whilst each set of questions relates to the subject of the chapter, all the questions need to be answered before you can usefully go on to define the elements that make up the Brand Arrow. For example, by reading the chapter on brand proposition you will not be able to immediately write your own one. You will, of course, learn about its role, and how to develop a positioning, and how it fits into your brand strategy. But you need to have been through all the elements of the brand strategy before you do. The reason for this is that although the process is a series of steps, it's iterative, so the answer you give in, say, step six may well mean you need to go back and reconsider step five.

It's up to you how and when you approach the questions - you can answer them on your own or with your team, at the end of each chapter or when you have finished the book. Either way, you'll have all you need to complete your Brand Arrow. In the final chapter, there is a guide to how to use the questions as a framework to build your own Brand Arrow. Oh, it's worth mentioning here that, of course, you don't have to answer any of these questions to get value from this book – I very much hope that just by reading it you'll come across insights you can apply to your own organization.

The questions

For now, I'd ask you to consider the following when approaching the questions.

When I develop a brand strategy for a client, I have in mind I'm writing for an intelligent but uninformed individual, so I always do my best to avoid jargon and use clear language that doesn't rely on industry knowledge. It may seem odd, given the client obviously is informed and will know their sector backward.

However, I find it a useful discipline because by avoiding jargon I have to state clearly what I want to communicate and not rely on short cuts that the reader may or may not understand. It also provides a chance to look at an issue or opportunity from an outside point of view, which in my experience can often reveal themes that can go unnoticed when you're "in the weeds". It's also very useful when you want to re-use elements of the brand strategy, say for website copy or a design brief. So, I suggest when you are answering these Brand Arrow questions you try and limit the jargon, or if you can't, perhaps define sector-specific language you will be using, and always do your best to write in a way that will be clear to any reader.

You will notice the Brand Arrow questions often ask for an exact number of things – write one sentence or list five characteristics, for example. It's a practice I use when working with clients to encourage them to process information before providing an answer – it's an easy way to start to get to hierarchies instead of creating long, shapeless lists. It will be helpful for you to try and limit your answers as directed – or as my mum used to say to me before an exam: make sure you answer the question!

Final point: I have written the book so that you don't need me; if you follow the plan I have no doubt you'll be able to create and shoot your own Brand Arrow. As a purchaser of this book, you will be able to download the Brand Arrow workshop chart from my website, **www.brucemmckinnon.com**, by entering the ISBN code found at the start of the book.

1. BRAND
An Exploration of What the Term Actually Means

THE KEY MESSAGES IN THIS CHAPTER:

- Brand strategy is a framework for you to make good choices.

- It forces you to prioritize what's really important.

- It's for every department, not just marketing.

At its simplest, branding is a way of claiming ownership, identifying the maker, providing an assurance of quality, and a means of distinguishing from other similar products. And branding has been around for a while. We know that the Egyptians as far back as 2700 BC[1] used fire-heated implements to mark their cattle to signify ownership – something that continued for centuries; even today some livestock are swabbed with a color for identification purposes.

The branding of products had to wait of course until there were products to brand. At the time of the Romans, with goods spread across the empire, the name and provenance of the producers were displayed via a stamp on the pottery vessels or painted onto ceramics, for example. In China, back in 960 AD, one of the first recorded brands was called White Rabbit Needles and came complete with logo and a very cool slogan – *ready to use at home in no time.*[2] In the UK, makers' marks on bread became compulsory in the 13th century and branding silver (through hallmarks) was required in the 14th century,[3][4] but the biggest change came in the 18th century with the advent of the industrial revolution.

Broadly up to this point, things were made by local people, quite often by hand, and sold to local people. Production reflected what the maker could produce and what the locals could consume. With the advent of the industrial revolution came the capacity to manufacture vast numbers of items, all of which needed to find vast numbers of customers to sell to – and very often these customers were a great distance from where the products were made. So you could no longer pop round to Bob's if you found a weevil in the bag of flour he sold you. Products made in Birmingham were being consumed all over the world and its provenance needed to be communicated, and as the market grew, the products needed to be distinguished from one another.

This ushered in what we now think of as modern brands, with products from all kinds of producers and countries using brand names, imagery, slogans, packaging and publicity to communicate their quality credentials and their distinctiveness from other brands. This was a significant change and reflected a society that had moved from seeking its needs to be met, to seeking choice. The role of the brand, in turn, has moved from a guarantee that a product is safe and can be trusted (this bag of flour has no weevils), to one that captures why the brand believes it's better or distinct from other similar brands (our flour is the purest/most refined/ cheapest, etc.).

Fast forward to today and on a trip to the supermarket you'll find as much as 45,000[5] products in store, and a visit to the US Amazon website will provide you with 12 million[6] products to choose from! Yes, not every product is a separate brand but you get the idea. Brands are part of our everyday life; they allow companies to communicate with us and provide us with the means of making a choice – even if in reality there is little tangible difference between brands in the same category.

In this chapter we are going to define some of the terms that swirl around the subject, look at the role brand strategy can play in an organization and finally, spend some time considering that brand strategy demands choices to be made about what is and is not the point of your organization.

The meaning of brand

If every team member has an understanding of the brand and what it stands for, and if that understanding is applied to their specific role, and pervades their products and services, then the customer will be delivered a consistent experience of that organization every single time they interact with it. This consistency is not only good for the customer, it's good for the organization as it ensures its assets are used as efficiently as possible, knowing that their next product, campaign or sponsorship deal will support the way the brand is seen by the world.

However, the term "brand" can mean many things. It can mean a product, a company, even a logo, and if you do settle on one of those terms there is no universal definition of the word brand, which is ironic given one of the roles of a brand is to deliver clarity. Being clear is very important for a brand, and it's very important for this book, so given there is no standard definition, I have made up my own set of definitions, which use everyday language, and are straightforward and appropriate for the purposes of this book.

A "brand" is a product or a service that delivers a consistent and distinctive benefit to a customer. It will contain a set of characteristics that it will use to differentiate itself from its competitors and ensure it remains relevant to its customers.

OK, that's brand done, but of course, this book is about brand strategy, so we need a definition for that too, and again there are many versions and most seem to be quite involved and complex. I don't believe a brand strategy has to be complex, nor does it need an expert to create one, it is simply ordering your thinking into a framework that allows you to shape your organization around delivering your point.

A "brand strategy" is a framework for you to make good choices. It prioritizes the purpose and character of your brand. Its role is to inspire and equip the brand owner to make the best decisions in the delivery of the brand to its customers.

To complete the trilogy, let's define the term "branding". I am often introduced as the consultant helping an organization with its branding. I have to confess this vexes me a little because of course I'm hired to consult on brand strategy, not branding. The two are different, as branding is an expression of the brand strategy; it comes once the strategy has been defined. However, before that vexation expresses itself and ruins a good relationship I pull myself together and say yes, I'm the branding guy, knowing that by the end of my assignment there will be no such confusion!

"Branding" uses a combination of words, colors and graphic images to communicate the brand strategy in a way that will engage the brand with its customers.

"Think of the brand strategy as the DNA of an organization."

There will be plenty more variations on the above that you can look up, but for our purposes, these three will do. However, all of them rely on truth. Claiming to be one thing and delivering another will not result in a strong brand; customers will find you out and most likely move to a brand that is authentic. The book is about harnessing that truth, giving it a shape (i.e. a point) and applying that point to how the brand can communicate.

The role of brand strategy

Your DNA is what makes you uniquely you – it defines the fundamental and distinctive characteristics of all living things, and I find it helpful to think of the brand strategy as the DNA of an organization. Just as DNA holds a set of instructions for the body that determine its characteristics, the brand strategy holds a set of instructions that determine the character of an organization. Those instructions will define the single most important thing about an organization, its character and its values. Furthermore, DNA has a clear structure and so too does a brand strategy, with each element within it having a specific role. However, the most compelling reason for comparing the two is that DNA informs every part of the body, and so a brand strategy's role should be to shape and direct how different aspects of an organization behave.

Brand strategy is quite often introduced to an organization through the marketing function, and its first iterations are usually created by the marketing team. However, its role cannot be confined to that department alone or it will fail. There's little point in creating a set of messages based on a brand strategy if the product or service those messages represent is not informed by that same strategy. Similarly, espousing a set of values to customers that do not also shape the organization they come from will be quickly dismissed as meaningless by those same customers. A management team that demands the highest level of integrity from its staff but does not embody that integrity in its own actions will be discredited. The brand strategy can, therefore, be seen as the mechanism that binds the organization together, both in its shared purpose and the means by which that purpose is pursued. And a very good way to try to make that happen is to ensure the whole organization is represented in the development of the brand strategy.

With my own client work, I have a process that engages stakeholders from all parts of the organization through interviewing key team members and holding workshops to elicit their views. Not only does this provide the insights needed to shape the strategy, it also creates a shared ownership; in effect, "it's not the consultant's brand strategy, it's ours". So it's important therefore to be intentional in sharing the recommended strategy with the team – not so that it can be changed, but to allow each team member a chance to "kick its tires". This can be done simply by presenting the brand strategy at a team meeting and using it as a framework to start to plan the next set of goals and objectives.

As we work through the book you will find that the brand strategy can become a very useful tool in providing cohesion and direction in the way the organization develops and expresses its services. For example, it can shape things like:

- the benefits and features across the product or service portfolio;

- the focus of sales messaging for those products and services;

- the presentation of the brand across marketing channels like the website and brochures;

- the way in which suppliers and partners are engaged and managed;

- the overt response from the management team in getting behind it;

- and finally, and most importantly, the commitment to honor the promises made to customers.

> *"The brand needs to sit above the minutiae of the organization, because it has to be relevant to every part of it."*

This is not to "big up" the brand strategy – it can be a very light touch for some teams and more pervasive for others – but it is simply an acknowledgment that if the brand strategy is to be influential and, like DNA, shape the character of the organization, then it needs to be put into the hands of the people who will actually create and deliver the brand. This is why the brand needs to sit above the minutiae of the organization, because it has to be relevant to every part of it.

Brand strategy is an exercise in choice

Most often when I begin my in-depth interviews with clients at the start of the development process, I ask the respondent to tell me what the point of their organization is. This is not an easy question to answer. I know this because I usually get back, after a long pause, something like, "This is not an easy question to answer." I then get told that it all depends on what product I am asking about, or the customer type, or the regions they are operating in, or the time of year, and it goes on.

None of these points are wrong, and, later in the process, each will play a significant role in deciding how to develop the best set of product features, what messaging to create, what channel to send those messages down. But that is for later; first we have to define what the point of the brand is, and the reason I start with that question is that it mirrors the first question a customer will ask the brand – in effect, why should I care about you? What is your point? What the brand cannot do is to respond with a series of qualifying questions.

Let's say I was sitting in front of Apple's CEO and I ask him that same question. I would not get back a series of questions about whether I was interested in the iPod 4 or the iPhone XS or the MacBook Pro. No, what I would get back, I would imagine, would be something along the lines of Apple's point is to design technology so intuitive that it becomes an extension for your own creativity. (By the way, that's my opinion as a user, I didn't look it up!)

The purpose of that tricky first question is not to get the answer there and then, but to get the client to start to think about how the brand might communicate its overall point. And that I suppose is my point – the brand strategy process should drive us up and above the details of the product benefits and features to be able to see the overall benefit that the brand delivers. This is especially important as digital technology is blurring traditional ways of defining brands; who, for example, would now describe Amazon as an online bookstore! So the job of a brand strategy, first of all, is to provide direction to the internal team, direction that can be relevant to any role with any product in the market. It has to be as understandable and directional to the HR team as it is to the product team as it is to the warehouse team.

So, looking back to the first question, once I have convinced the respondent that it is entirely possible to sum the brand up in a sentence, I always get very instructive, if very different, answers (I usually do around 15 of these interviews). It shows me where the key stakeholders, at least in their own heads, place the value they see the brand delivering. It is also an excellent way to start to introduce the idea that a brand is largely about exerting choice, because with one sentence you can't say too much, so what will you choose to say, and as importantly, what will choose to leave out?

So, a great deal of developing a brand strategy is about making choices, because if you make the choices in the strategic development phase, then you stop the organization, or the agency, or the product manager potentially making the wrong choices at the execution stage.

Once that question is answered I usually follow up with the invitation to pick a single word to sum up the brand. This is an equally unpopular question! Again, it's simply an early exploration of where the most influential people in the organization feel the brand's value is. Of course, in my own client process and in this book, the answer does not come in the first one or two questions, it will come as we go through the process, learning as we go what the truths of the brand are and the demands placed on it by its customers.

Case study: Orange is not a color

On 28 April 1994, the world changed forever.

OK, not the whole world but the brand world, because that's when Orange was launched in the UK.[7] It did so with an ad showing a floating baby to a soundtrack from the excellent Phillip Glass with the promise of a brighter, wire-free future.

Orange was, in fact, one of the first brands that put attitude before hardware and launched into a market that was transactional in nature with brands like Vodafone (short for voice and data phone) and BT Cell Net (BT Cellular Network) dominating the market.

However, this was not just style above substance, the brand needed to back up this new view of the world and its future with things that would genuinely differentiate it from the well-heeled and well-established competition. It did so by positioning itself as a friend to the customer in a whole host of ways; the most significant initially was the commitment to only charge its customers for the time they spent on their calls.

Whilst that seems obvious now, back in the mid 90s the mobile operators all rounded up to the nearest minute. So if you made a 20-second call, you would be charged for the full minute. Not fair, but that was how the customers were treated. And the move from Orange, known as Per Second Billing,[8] meant that whilst it generated less revenue, it gained enormously by winning the trust of its customers. It did not take long for the incumbents to follow suit. Per Second Billing was the first of many initiatives that told the customer that the Orange brand had a different point of view that shaped how it engaged with its customers.

Another example concerns the user manuals for handsets, which were notoriously long, complex and frankly hard to understand. Orange re-wrote every single one so that its customers could understand how the phone worked – so instead of the Nokia 6210 manual, customers would get the Orange Nokia 6210 manual, which would usually start with the word "hello". There were costs to Orange as it meant it very often had to launch new handsets later than its competition because the manuals needed rewriting and printing. The benefit, of course, was that Orange customers felt they were being treated in a way that was unique.

Another distinctive aspect to Orange was its advertising – I'm not referring to that floating baby from the launch ad, no, it's that you would never see a handset in an Orange ad. This reflected their belief that people were buying into the brand, and that the handset, whilst important, was secondary.

But the world was catching up with Orange and in 2002, O2 and T-Mobile were launched, with Three (the new brand from the former owners of Orange) following in 2003. The fusty old transactional brands were being put out to pasture and replaced with new brands that benefited from Orange's pioneering work.

And that's when I stepped into the hallowed halls of Orange to work with the CEO to develop a strategy to fend off these new and well-funded competitors. It was during this time we found a problem with the brand – a problem caused by its success.

Because it was so successful, and its branding so distinctive, many of the teams working at Orange felt because they knew the brand so well, and because their customers did too, adherence to the brand guidelines (in effect the brand's own user manual) had become less important.

What it meant was dozens of slightly different expressions of the Orange brand, depending on the agency or the division responsible for it. And slightly different expressions of the brand meant that overall it had become disjointed, much like a jigsaw with pieces that didn't quite fit together.

So the issue was not about the brand, it was about the culture, and the need for the teams across the organization to re-engage with the truths and purpose of the brand again – to re-learn what the brand existed for and its role with customers.

To address this we created Step Change, a program with the entire senior management team to first of all re-engage them in the brand strategy, and then to work through how to face the forthcoming challenge, drawing on the principles of the brand as the main response. Orange succeeded in this difficult time not by changing its brand but by recommitting to it, and then ensuring the whole company got behind it.

Fast forward to today and the brand operates successfully in 27 countries, but ironically not in the UK.[9] It is true to say Orange ushered in a new era of brands and you can still see its effect today – Sky Mobile allowing customers to keep their unused data instead of it disappearing at the end of the month[10] is a very "Orange" idea, as is O2 allowing customers to break free of long-term contracts in order to get a new phone when they want instead of having to wait out their contract.

So the future is still bright, and for 27 countries, it's still Orange!

BRAND ARROW QUESTIONS

BA1: Name the three key themes that characterize the sector you are in.

How would you capture the character of the sector, field, industry, etc. that you are in? Is it a sector that has gone through significant change in the last five years? If so, what has driven that change? A new entrant? Technology? Consumer behavior? Perhaps your sector hasn't changed at all and you are looking to shake things up? Or maybe a new brand has changed the dynamics of the sector? What kind of companies do you compete with? Are they all pretty much the same with only small differences separating them, or maybe there are fundamental differences in what each one offers. Aim to write three paragraphs, one for each theme.

BA2: What is the single most pressing need the sector is meeting and how might that change over time?

What do your customers want? What needs are you meeting? For example, getting legal expertise but without having to hire a lawyer, or the need to eat more healthily without it taking longer to source and prepare meals. Try and sum up the major need, or problem, the sector solves for its customers now. Once you are done, explore where the trends might be taking the sector and state what its needs might be in five and ten years.

2. WHY BRAND IS IMPORTANT
The Point of Having a Point

THE KEY MESSAGES IN THIS CHAPTER:

- A brand is an asset that can be valued.

- Brands play a vital role in customers' decision making.

- Brands save an organization time and money.

Shipping containers. Very clever. At the last count there's over 20 million[11] of them circulating around the world, and what makes them very useful is they all share the same dimensions so can be fitted on a ship, a train or a truck - you can even stack them too. That means a container can be placed on a ship in Japan, sail over to San Francisco where it's put on a train down to San Diego, before being loaded onto a truck to go down to Los Mochis in Mexico where it's unloaded and stacked with other containers in readiness for its next journey. It all fits. It's amazing, and the reason it's possible is ISO 6346, issued between 1968 and 1970, containing the global standard dimensions for shipping containers.[12]

ISO stands for International Standards Organization. Set up in 1947 and based in Geneva, its aim is to help the world function more easily and safely by developing and publishing standards across everything from agricultural products, currency and medical devices to telephone country codes and health and safety standards. In fact, it has issued over 20,000 standards,[13] and for us brand strategists, ISO 10668, published in 2010, is of great interest as it lays out the requirements for the procedures and methods of measuring the value of a brand.[14]

But how do you value something like a name, a set of values, a campaign, that by definition is intangible? This chapter explores how brands are valued and the benefits a brand delivers to customers and the organizations that own them.

How a brand is valued

ISO defines the term brand as an intangible asset (as opposed to tangible assets like machinery, buildings and inventory); a non-financial asset with no physical substance[15] – we are talking logos, symbols, names, values, etc. The reason why ISO felt the need to create a common method for valuing these intangible assets is that they are worth vast sums of money. For example, according to Forbes, in 2018, the Apple brand was valued at $182.8bn. That's around 20 percent of the total net worth of the whole company.[16] So, how does ISO go about valuing something that you can't get hold of? Very carefully.

First, like all the items it measures, ISO provides a precise definition of what a brand is – it's very thorough and very long, and as we already have a useful definition I'm not including it here. It then defines what the purpose of the valuation is – it may aid internal planning, inform a prospective purchase or be needed for tax and compliance reasons, for example. This is significant as different purposes will give different valuations – what ISO refers to as the Promise of Value. Once done there are three different methods to define value:

- Income, which measures the earnings the brand could generate in the future.

- Market, which compares the brand to the value of similar brands in the market.

- Cost, which captures either the cost of building the brand or the cost of replacing it.[17]

I'm paraphrasing here, but this is broadly the process, and once completed, there is the need to make sure that all the inputs are objective and reliable. Finally, it all goes into a Valuation Report that details the valuation itself and all the steps taken in the process.

There are other methods and other organizations providing valuations; the point here is to simply say that brands have enormous value and there are objective and well-established methods for measuring that value.

It's worth noting that not every company will have a brand that makes up a significant proportion of their total financial value. To a great degree, it depends on how engaged a customer will be in the brand experience. For Apple, the brand and the device are wedded together and so every time we handle the device we are in effect handling the brand (on average we will pick up our smartphone over 50 times a day).[18] An organization that has a low touch-brand experience, like a spark plug company, for example, where we don't handle the product but enjoy its benefits through other brands (like our cars), the brand's contribution to the overall value of the company will be significantly less.

Why customers value brands

Sticking with our friends from ISO, let's look at the example of the painkiller ibuprofen, which has a set of standardized ingredients (ISO/IEC 17025),[19] which means, of course, that a pack in Copenhagen will contain the same ingredients as a pack bought in Lima. Interestingly, by introducing a brand into the equation, the cost of buying what is essentially an identical product can vary wildly – a trip to the local store revealed a pack of 16 branded tablets costs over six times the amount for a pack of unbranded tablets.[20]

And to be clear, there is no tangible difference between the branded and unbranded versions. An article by Saleyha Ahsan in the *Guardian* newspaper in 2016[21] reported on an experiment at University College London that sought to discover if the brand leader ibuprofen was more effective than an unbranded ibuprofen. In short, the effectiveness of the unbranded and the branded tablet was identical. So, how can a branded product that does the exact same job as an unbranded product charge so much more, and just as importantly, why should a customer be willing to pay so much extra?

Well, it's back to the idea of intangibility. Although Saleyha Ahsan's ibuprofen experiment proved the results were the same, customers in my local store were clearly willing to pay substantially more for the branded version.

There are a number of reasons for this, and one of the most pervasive is around the fact that brands, rightly or wrongly, deliver an assurance they can be trusted. In this instance, it may be that the customer has always bought that particular brand, or it was always in the bathroom cabinet growing up at home, or their experience of using the brand has been good. Whatever the reason there is a familiarity with the brand that delivers trust. So when considering their choice, the customer plumps for the one that they are familiar with. There are countless research studies that confirm that customers trust branded products more than they trust unbranded products.

This act of choice ironically is something most brand owners would rather not happen. Instead, they want their customers to sort of shop on autopilot, with their brand already firmly in their mind. I have first-hand experience of the idea of shopping on autopilot. Saturdays mean my daughter has a two-hour gymnastics class in the neighboring town and I use that time to buy the weekly groceries. I can do the shop in a very racy 30 minutes, giving me a comfortable hour or so at the coffee bar across the road to read the weekend papers. I rarely miss items and get very few complaints from my family about my choices. I like this Saturday routine and it is me on autopilot that allows it to happen.

The brain manages to screen out the vast amount of stimuli we receive every day, and of that stimuli we are increasingly bombarded with brands and advertising – various research studies put the number of ads we see on a daily basis from 4,000 through to 10,000.[22] That's mind-boggling and our brain does an excellent job in screening out the bulk of them. But it knows when a brand comes along I like and lets that one through. So on my Saturday shop, I may pause to look at the 20 different kinds of butter on the shelves but I'm only "seeing" my brand – into the trolley it goes and my autopilot directs me to the next favored brand choice. It goes without saying that being one of the brands a customer carries around in their head is extremely valuable for brand owners.

This is not to say that brands do not have tangible benefits and features that mark them out against either unbranded products or brands they are competing with. Indeed most brands are built on the promise of a better, different or a distinctive experience. Most often (but not always) better means higher quality and a higher price. A branded butter may well command a higher price and possibly deliver a better quality product than a tub of unbranded butter. A premium brand may be seen as better than a standard brand, which in turn may be seen as better than a budget brand, etc. Each category will have a sort of strata within it that will first help a customer make a choice that suits them and their budget and then act as a guide for the customer to "see" it in the grocery store or in the media.

Brands might also charge a premium not just for offering a better product, but a different product. That could be a feature that appeals to a particular customer – instant coffee with half the caffeine, a car built for off-road driving, for example. And then there are many product areas that are basically the same, so the role of the brand here is to discover and embody a distinctiveness that will mark them out and appeal to a particular customer. A great many sectors fall into this category – fashion and alcoholic drinks, for example.

"The brands we consume say something about us and our capacity to choose."

Finally, it's worth pointing out that to a greater or lesser degree we have some notion that the brands we consume say something about us and our capacity to choose. This informs the clothes we wear, the cars we drive, the drinks we order, even the street we want to live on, etc. Brands signal to the world an image we project – intentionally or not. And brand owners rely on this because they know that customers are willing to pay a substantial premium for products that enhance or reinforce their self-image. As long as the brand maintains its standing, this dynamic becomes self-generating as the premium paid goes to support the brand's efforts to maintain its position, which allows the brand to remain in the customer's minds, or be visible when the customers is ready to make a choice.

Why organizations value brands

We can see that the brand plays a vital role in engaging and keeping in the minds of its customers, in supporting efforts to grow sales, and providing clear signals to its customers about the value it delivers. And that role, through a variety of well-established processes, can also be measured in financial value.

So the benefits of having a strong brand are clear.

Externally, customers can recognize the products it represents and are often willing to pay more for them. The brand provides a means of expressing what makes it relevant to customers and different from the competition. It's also the conduit for engaging its customers through media – whether that's a post on Instagram, an ad on TV or promotion on the pack, all will use the messaging, colors, logo and imagery that communicate the brand. The brand ensures all this different activity is consistently presented which means that the investment made in media is used as efficiently as possible.

Internally, the brand provides a focus for the team, it represents a distillation of its features and benefits into a clear hierarchy, it will ensure that messaging to customers can be easily and quickly developed based on those features and benefits, it ensures that every part of the organization knows the direction it is headed. This means, for example, that new products will enhance and extend the brand, the organization's culture will reflect the brand values, and that the sales team will have the resources needed to hit their targets. All this reduces the chance of costly mistakes and ensures that an organization's resources are used as effectively as possible.

For a global brand this will mean each country has a clear idea about what the brand stands for, its key benefits and features, and how it should be marketed, for example, and this saves time and money. Instead of every country developing its own marketing campaigns, each can either draw from material developed centrally or it can develop its own campaign based on the established brand.

A local brand can also enjoy those kinds of benefits. For example, a restaurant opening in a second venue in the next town will base the experience it wants to deliver on the first restaurant because it knows it works and it would be counterproductive to develop something new. A company pitching for a new contract will reference its success to date; it will present its key benefits, the features that deliver those benefits, and the proof that it is effective. It may only appear on a PowerPoint presentation but it is still drawing from the brand.

All of these benefits also have the potential to deliver cost savings. For example, if the organization has to devote management time to develop key messaging when it develops a new campaign this will take up valuable resource and may well deliver an inconsistent campaign. However, if through the brand strategy process that key messaging is already established, the management knows the campaign will be in line with the organization's direction, it will be able to be created quickly and will be consistent with previous work. Organizations that operate global brands can save money by, for example, developing a new product for all their markets and not each market developing their own, or creating advertising through one agency for all markets and not dozens of different agencies creating dozens of different campaigns.

So why doesn't everybody have a brand? Well, all brands are not equal and the best of those take time and resources to build. For example, Apple's investment in advertising in 2015 (the last year it revealed its figures) was $1.8bn.[23] However, for most of us, whilst we won't be seeking ISO's methodology

> *"A strong brand does deliver benefits to its owners, and a brand comes from a brand strategy."*

for valuing a brand just yet or allocating resources to advertising, we do need to recognize that a strong brand does deliver benefits to its owners, and a brand comes from a brand strategy. Yes, in some cases that strategy may have initially been intuitive and informal, in other cases it would have been the result of an intentional process, but either way, to get the most value from your brand there needs to be a structure in place to ensure the brand is authentic (the roots and expression of those roots are true) and is being used correctly (how the brand is presented and used). Of course, the big brands out there – Nike, Levi's, Nescafé – will all have methods for maintaining their brands because of their immense value, but any brand, however small, needs to be able to define what it stands for and what it delivers to customers.

Case study: Hmmm, where does this go?

I think of the process of defining a point for a brand is a little like exploring a city. The only way to know if you are heading up a blind alley is go and have a look – you could end with a brick wall, or maybe you'll find yourself in a pretty little park with a burbling fountain, a bench to sit on and the sun to warm your face. And the only way to know if an idea has the potential to lead somewhere is to play it out, think it through, test it with the work you have done so far or share it with colleagues. Once ideas start to coalesce you can explore different options to express the point of the brand – some will work, some will not. That's OK because to develop a brand strategy is a process of exploration – better to do it in the strategic phase rather than when you are in the throes of designing a new brand identity, developing a marketing campaign or writing a press release.

I went for a bit of an explore in New York a few years ago with Barbara Cicatelli who had founded Cicatelli Associates Incorporated, known as

> *"Any brand, however small, needs to be able to define what it stands for and what it delivers to customers."*

CAI. Founded in 1979,[24] CAI is a pioneer in designing and delivering training to health and social service providers to better support marginalized members of society. Its focus is very much on using the transformative power of education and research to foster a more aware, healthy, compassionate world. Barbara was at the time thinking of how to transition the brand from an emphasis on her to one that focused more on the benefits her team delivered. During the brand strategy process we kept coming back to the fact that their focus on transformation was in effect a focus on change, and especially their commitment to equip and inspire others to make that change through its training programs.

But here's the rub. Although well known in their sector, the name CAI did not speak to the exciting idea at the center of their organization; it did nothing to communicate the point of their brand, or at least provide a useful stepping-stone to deliver their point. But we were stuck with those initials and just had to make them work. So that's when we started to explore and found ourselves looking down an alley whose name began with the letter C. C for CAI. And C for Change. Hmmm. How about we change what the initials stand for? From Cicatelli Associates Incorporated to something that lets people know what Barbara and her team deliver – to make the door to their services as wide as possible, to capture the point of their business in the name of the brand.

OK, so we have Change – the positioning of the organization – as the first word, but what about their need to equip and inspire others through their training programs? What a minute – Inspiration, that takes care of the initial I. Yoke the two words together and you come to CAI: Change and Inspiration. This repurposing of the name allowed Barbara and her team to capture the essence of the organization in three words that would always appear with their initials and provide a fresh and exciting way of coupling their name to their mission. And, of course, in doing so we delivered the point of their brand.

BRAND ARROW QUESTIONS

BA3: What three brands, from any field, strike a chord with you? Why?

We have all grown up with these intangible assets called brands, some we like, and some we don't, some we remember from childhood, some have just been created. And whilst we can argue about how much time we consciously engage with them, it's fair to say that we could probably sit down right now and list fifty of them.

For this question, pick three brands that you know well and try and sum up what the brand is about. You could jot down what the brand stands for, why it's better than others in its sector, it doesn't matter, just take some time to think about what the story of the brand is.

BA4: Name your three most successful competitors. List the reasons why you think they are successful.

Moving to your own sector, it's very helpful to have a look at your competitors. We will be exploring this more closely in chapter 12, but for now, make a list of the three you think are doing well and make a note of why you think that is. A good website? A low price point? A clever business model? What can you learn from them? If you had to distil a single thing that makes them who they are, what would it be? This is important because it's both helpful to learn how others offer similar products or services to you, and, of course, when you develop your own brand strategy you need to be sure it's distinctive.

CUSTOMER

POSITIONING

PROPOSITION

VALUES

PROBLEM

SOLUTION

BENEFITS

FEATURES

DISTINCTION

VISION

VISION

Defining and guiding the
brand to its destination

3. VISION
Defining Your Destination

THE KEY MESSAGES IN THIS CHAPTER:

- You can only make progress if you know where you are going.

- Everybody needs to be on board with the vision.

- Identify the drivers and barriers to you getting there.

On 25 May 1961, in the middle of a cold war, the US was losing ground in the space race to Russia. In a bid to catch up and overtake their rivals President Kennedy committed himself and the whole country to get a man on the moon by the end of the decade.[25] It was a gargantuan and ambitious project. However, with the combined impact of billions of NASA dollars and JFK's charismatic leadership, it was seen as possible.

The following year, on a tour of the NASA HQ, JFK came upon a janitor sweeping the floor, and on asking what his job was the janitor replied, "Mr President, I'm sending a man to the moon."[26] The vision for the program had been successfully defined and communicated. Everybody at HQ shared a sense of the ambition of the organization. A vision's role is to bring the whole organization together by understanding what their shared ambition or destination is. And to get excited about it!

In this chapter, we are going to look at what a vision statement is and how you can put one together that manages to be both instructional and inspirational. We'll explore what can go into a vision statement, what kind of response it should illicit, and the role it will play, particularly with the team charged with delivering the brand. We'll look at a number of vision statements, and whilst all have the same job of creating excitement and purpose amongst the team, all go about it in different ways. We will then go on to look at how practically the brand strategy can equip the organization to start to move toward that vision.

Where do you want to end up?

At the age of 21, I joined three friends on a three-month, 10,000 mile trip from Edinburgh down to Zimbabwe. We drove over the high altitude passes of the Atlas Mountains, across the hot-as-a-furnace Sahara desert, into the muddy wet rainforests of the Congo, and through the vast plateaus of Zambia before arriving in Zimbabwe. Knowing where we were headed meant we knew we had to make the right preparations: we bought an old but reliable Land Rover which we fitted with spare fuel and water canisters, we each trained to be able to perform our specifics roles, and we planned the route as carefully as we could. We made it in one piece with a few stories to tell.

We could not have done the trip in a Toyota Corolla. Knowing the destination meant we were able to be equipped and prepared.

"For a resource as potent as the brand to play a role in equipping the organization to get to its destination, it first needs to know where that is."

When I'm working with clients I often refer to the need to define their vision as a need to define their destination, because the job of the brand strategy is to help the organization get there. For a resource as potent as the brand to play a role in equipping the organization to get to its destination, it first needs to know where that is. If your vision is to be "the best-known brand in the world", the brand strategy will have a different approach than if you were creating a niche brand to serve a small number of customers.

Of course, progress toward a vision cannot be made without first defining what that vision is. And the process of developing a brand strategy is a great way to engage the team in exploring what your vision might be - where you want to end up. This can then be presented in an accessible and inspirational way for the team, shareholders, suppliers and customers. The brand strategy is a response to the vision, and it will usually come as the first thing your team will see when you reveal your strategy, so it needs to be authentic, inspiring, a place where you can acknowledge your faults and make a commitment to put them right. And because you will have developed it with your team, there will be a sense of a shared effort and commitment to make that vision a reality.

The vision, however, should be high level. There is no benefit in spending time and resource defining the exact destination because by the time you get there – if you get there – it may have all changed! Our successful plan to reach Zimbabwe was not contingent on knowing the exact street address or the local map of Harare. We needed to know the general direction and what we would need to overcome on the way.

I thought it would be helpful to give you a sense of some actual vision statements so here are some excerpts from a variety of my clients.

We want to be a thought leader in the IT sector by applying an open mind, expert knowledge and a breadth of experience to deliver solutions based solely on their ability to solve a problem. And nothing else. Within four years, to grow to around 200 people, spread over four geographical hubs, maintaining a high level of senior consultant-client interactions. To be able to realize this growth by creating appropriate infrastructure and systems as well as reinvesting profits in staff, the organization, sales and marketing. (Software company)

Our vision is to work in partnership with clients to attract, develop and retain the highest caliber of talent, who will one day shape the future of business. To do this we will asses and develop undergraduate to mid-career candidates, foster their progress to leadership positions and build long-term retained relationships with clients. In so doing we will contribute to the development and retention of our client's employees by shaping their talent and organizational strategies and program. (Recruitment agency)

We believe in a world where every woman has a range of choice unbound by her size. Where she has the confidence to express herself in as many ways as she pleases. Where we are her most trusted ally, dedicated to crafting the most comfortable, stylish and supportive bras. Because in our world, every woman deserves a bra that fits. (Lingerie company)

We believe in the power of widening access to expertise and aim to become the global standard for any organization in any sector committed to delivering that access. We will deliver that belief by offering the best technology in the world for building, deploying and maintaining automated expertise solutions, and in doing so, will make a positive and lasting impact on society. (Automation company)

Our dream is to help create a world where people live a healthier and happier life - one not marred by weight problems and low self-esteem. To change people's lives by instilling the importance of healthy living and eating. We want to make a real difference to people's lives: to motivate, equip and empower everyone who wants to lose weight and adopt a healthier lifestyle. (Healthy eating brand)

We want to move from a trusted transactional supplier to an influential and essential business partner delivering value to clients on a global stage. To be the first place business leaders turn to for support and direction to face any opportunity the future may hold. To make this transition in a credible and timely way, building on our assets and better expressing our existing strategic expertise. (Data center)

You will have seen from the above that vision statements cannot follow a set framework as they will be tailored to a unique set of circumstances and will need to be absolutely wedded to your brand. Some will include a challenge you are facing and the need to rise up to meet it; others may focus on a changing sector and how it calls for new thinking; others could acknowledge past mistakes or focus on the strength of your services that may have been forgotten. All, however, will define what success looks like and avoid using technical jargon because everybody in the organization needs to first understand the vision and second be excited by it.

Equipping the organization to get there

Once we had decided to make the trip to Zimbabwe we were then able to take stock of our ability to actually get there. This took no time at all as we were totally unprepared, and so began a process to ensure we were able to make the trip. We had to raise the funds to buy the equipment, define what type of equipment to buy, customize our Land Rover, apply for visas, get our vaccinations and most importantly get permission from our mums – we were all only 21 remember!

For you, once the vision is defined (the Brand Arrow questions will provide a useful framework) you can start to see what you have that will help you get there. Think of it as an audit of your capabilities. Unlike my 21-year-old self, you will already have a number of assets you can use, and if you are a start-up your new business idea would have come from your experience, connections, imagination and of course a willingness to work 20 hour days for peanuts. All of these are assets!

Start off by looking inside your organization. What do you have that you can use? For example, you might have a deep expertise in your sector, a product that is a leader in its class, or a website that has great content. I sometimes ask clients to make a distinction between assets that can immediately be used, and assets that need to be adapted. In effect, what do you have to build on and what do you need to build up; what can be used today and what needs a little work. Then look outside: what is going to help the brand move toward the vision? It may be there is increasing demand for your product or service, perhaps publicity to highlight a need or new regulations have come into force. It

"Once the vision is defined, you can start to see what you have that will help you get there."

may be that public opinion is creating a groundswell of interest in what you provide. I usually call these drivers as they will propel you toward your destination.

And if it is useful to know your strengths it is even more useful to know your weaknesses. If you are to start to move toward your vision you need to know what will slow you down and what is going to stop you – what barriers will need to be overcome. For example, your product may have lost its class leader position, your team may operate in silos and not work together cohesively, your resources may be stretched over too many products. Once done, look at the external factors that could stop you: a well-funded competitor, changing customer buying habits, a disruption to your supply chain. Contrary to what it may appear, I always find this an extremely positive process with clients as successfully solving a problem starts by recognizing there's a problem in the first place!

> *"Once you have identified your barriers and drivers you will have a mix of treasure and trouble."*

Once you have identified your barriers and drivers you will have a mix of treasure and trouble. The treasure – your drivers – needs to be put into an order of priority starting with the most effective driver, the most valuable asset you have in being able to reach your vision. Once you have, say, five drivers, work with your team to write a paragraph under each that describes how you can best leverage these drivers. It's a very useful exercise because as well as calling out your strengths, you are already doing the groundwork for developing key elements of your brand. For example, articulating your strengths will help define how you solve your customer's problem; your strengths will shape some of your brand values; you will be able to more easily create a message hierarchy that will feed into how you present your brand on your website, for example.

OK, that's the treasure, then you do the same for the trouble. Call out the biggest barriers – in effect, ask yourself what will stop the brand in its tracks, and then write a paragraph that covers what you can do to reduce or even remove them. For example, if it's silo-based working, systems could be put in place to ensure a more collegiate work environment, or the HR team could run a series of workshops on collaborative working practices. Once you have your list of five it will also become a valuable tool for the brand in its quest to support the organization in meeting its vision. In this case, it allows you to benchmark your progress against those issues and also ensures that the actions required to remedy them can be enshrined in your values. We will look at the idea of values as an antidote to your issues in chapter 6.

Tracking your progress

If you open up an atlas and look at the map of Algeria you'll see a number of yellow lines snaking across the Sahara that denote the road network. Do not believe it. There are no roads across the Sahara! Well, to be fair, that may have changed now but back on our trip in the mid 80s there were no roads to speak of. And of course no GPS. The only way of knowing if we were headed in the right direction was to follow a series of empty oil drums placed every kilometer or so along the route. Quite often though the drums were missing and so we resorted to our compass or asking the very, very occasional goat herder or camel rider where we were headed.

We would start our day before sunrise, at around 4.00 a.m., to try to make some progress before the heat took hold of the day. By 11.00 a.m., the Land Rover would start to overheat and it was simply too hot to think. We would stop, put up some shade, sit under it, reading and drinking hot tea (which we knew by some biological miracle reduced our body temperatures). I remember once our sojourn was rudely interrupted by a French expedition who came careening up to us in their rather newer Land Rover and shouted that we must be English as we were drinking tea in the midday sun!

It was important that we made progress because we only had a finite amount of fuel and water, and we would have genuinely been in danger had we failed to reach our destination. And so it is with our brand strategy journey, as now that we have defined a destination we need to make sure we are making progress toward reaching it. In effect, we need to set out our own oil drums to mark our own progress.

It won't be a revelation to you that I suggest that setting goals and objectives is useful. These terms can be interchangeable which can lead to confusion so when I'm working with clients I always refer to goals as a target to aim for and objectives as the activity needed to reach those targets. That means you will have fewer goals than objectives. Typically I aim for three goals and around three to five objectives for each. It is useful to plan these goals along short and medium-term periods, say 12 months and 36 months. If you are starting out or are planning major change, there is no reason why you can't set six monthly goals as it keeps the team on track and, importantly, will show early progress.

However, it's not enough to plan, you also have to know if you are delivering on that plan – so we need to measure progress. Typically, companies use Key Performance Indicators (KPIs) to do this, which is helpful if you have metrics you can measure like sales leads acquired or the number of articles written in the press. I also find it very helpful to use what I call Key Development Indicators (KDIs), which don't have a metric attached to them but reflect the need to achieve a certain objective, like recruit a new member of staff, hire a PR agency or create a new brand identity. These can be used interchangeably or together depending on the objectives. Here's an example:

Goal

Raise awareness of the brand as the leading provider of data services to the independent travel agency market.

Objective 1

- Develop and implement a comprehensive PR and media plan of activity.
- KDI: Hire a PR agency the first half of the calendar year.
- KPI: Ensure two articles are placed in the leading trade press every month in the second half of the calendar year.

Objective 2

- Develop an events strategy including national conferences and speaking opportunities.

- KPI: Generate 35 qualified leads from each event and 15 from attending each trade event.

- KDI: Attend six events, secure three speaking engagements for the CEO, host two customer events.

This happens to be from the marketing team, but every department should be able to put down a plan, using their own terms, to start to make progress toward a goal.

Case study: The Call

Based in Akron, Pennsylvania, Ten Thousand Villages (USA) is a fair trade retail chain that collaborates closely with communities in over thirty countries to design and create home decor items that are sold through their stores in North America. They pay a fair price, provide advance payment, are always in it for the long-term and endeavor to ensure every link in their supply chain is as ethical as possible.

It all started in 1946 when Edna Ruth Byler, travelling in Puerto Rico, was deeply struck by the challenges facing the rural communities living on the breadline. She was also struck by the beauty of the embroidery produced by the women of the region and realized that if she brought some of the pieces back home she was pretty sure she could sell them to friends and family. So that's what Ruth did. She saw that by providing a market to sell their wares, these communities could lift themselves out of poverty in a way that would be both dignified and sustainable. The Mennonite Central Committee, an aid and relief agency based in the same town, saw the power in this and supported her on trips to other parts of the world.

That relationship still holds today, and the organization has dozens of stores across the US and ships merchandise to hundreds more. Ruth pioneered a way of using trade to lift communities out of poverty that we now know as the fair trade movement. Over the years it became the market leader and sales continued to grow steadily, until the US recession of 2009. As the nation tightened its belt, sales dropped dramatically – after all, when money is tight, home decor items fall off the shopping list.

It took a number of years for the US economy to recover and this had a significant impact on the sales for Ten Thousand Villages. There was a need to rebuild the business, and the management team saw that along with a host of organizational measures, there was the need to leverage the values of the brand. In this instance, that meant harnessing all that the organization knew from the past and yoke it to a clear sense of future and so support the transformation of Ten Thousand Villages back to being a strong, authentic and inspirational leader.

The brand strategy played a role in this process in a number of ways, one of the most significant being a vision statement that provided a shared focus, and sense that all the team were headed in the same direction. The hope was that this focus along with the operational changes would inspire and start to shape new campaigns, product lines, new store layouts and a renewed sense of purpose. The vision statement, which we will go through now, started with an acknowledgment of past difficulties and then made a commitment to change. It then outlined how it was going to deliver those changes, and finally it defined the vision of Ten Thousand Villages. Interestingly, their vision has remained unchanged over the last three decades, it just needed to be reconnected to the people charged with making that vision a reality.

We named the vision "The Call" and it was used at the start of internal sessions to explore how the teams could use the brand strategy as a foundation for growing the sales and reconnecting to the brand and its values. Here it is:

The Call

These last few years, we have fallen short on what matters most to our artisans and our mission.

Orders

We sell significantly less now than we did 10 years ago. We buy significantly less now than we did 10 years ago.

Lacking in innovation and inspiration, we have been caught out by more nimble competitors. We have been saved from falling but we are still near the edge, unsure which direction we need to take.

We have fallen behind the movement we helped create.

But today this stops.

Today we will lift our heads up and say to the world that we have the audacity to believe we can successfully serve the poorest communities of the world through commerce.

Through our experience hewn from 70 years of sharing opportunities with artisans, we know we can deliver tangible, long-lasting impact and forge personal and valuable connections that will deliver a brighter and better future for us all.

To unite value and values, to create products for our customers, that in turn delivers benefits to our artisan partners and us. Benefits that are important – like income, sales and capacity building, and benefits that are transformational – like pride, dignity and purpose.

To practice commerce in an authentic and ethical way that liberates artisans from the shackles of poverty and customers from the tyranny of ignorance. And to do this we will once again take up the mantle of leadership, to be a beacon and guide for those we know and those we have yet to meet.

As a leader, we will guarantee a tangible and transformational impact – commercial and societal to all our communities. We will commit to creating an exchange of opportunity for artisans and customers that will deliver a personal and valued connection.

By doing this we can see a day when all artisans in developing countries will earn a fair wage, be treated with dignity and respect and be able to live a life of quality.

This is too important for us to fail.

Ten Thousand Villages (USA) had already turned a corner when this assignment was commissioned and I am glad to say their sales and market leadership is continuing to increase. The vision is not the reason for its progress, but it played a vital role in engaging and involving all the teams in the journey.

BRAND ARROW QUESTIONS

BA5: Where do you want to get to in 10 years (think big!)?

It's a big question and not easy to answer. When I talk to clients about what their vision might be I always start off by asking about where they want to be in 12 months. This deals with important but transactional stuff like, hire a new person for the sales team or re-do the website – and allows us to focus on the bigger picture. I usually then go on to ask about what the future looks like in three to five years before settling on the big question of ten years plus. This releases us from important practical issues and almost gives us permission to be able to dream a little. At this point, I would say not to get worried about making it sound eloquent, or perfectly written. The framework we are working on together is iterative, so once you have a broad idea about where you are headed you can focus on the next part of the process. Once you have a better idea about what your brand strategy is, you can come back if needs be and rewrite the vision to better reflect your strategy.

BA6: What will help you get there? What will slow you down?

Consider what drivers you have to help you get to that vision and what barriers might there be to slow you down or even stop you reaching it. For drivers, consider what your key strengths are, for example, you may have a product that is superior to the competition, your team might be highly skilled or there is a need in the market that your product clearly meets. For barriers, note down the issues you feel need to be resolved, for example, lack of internal communications that means the team works in silos, a product that is failing behind its competitors or a website that does not promote the brand as well as it could. Try to bullet point five barriers and drivers with a supporting paragraph under each bullet.

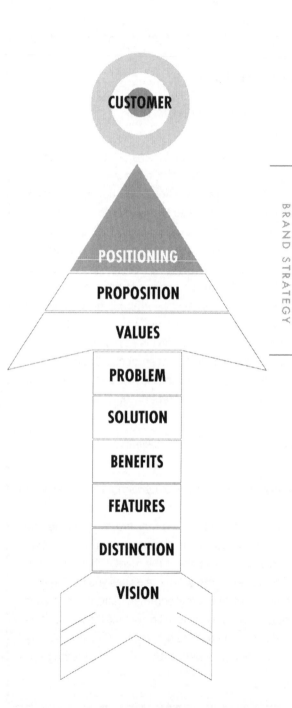

CUSTOMER

BRAND STRATEGY

POSITIONING

PROPOSITION

VALUES

One or two words that define the essence of the brand

PROBLEM

SOLUTION

BENEFITS

FEATURES

DISTINCTION

VISION

4. POSITIONING
Describing the Essence of the Brand

THE KEY MESSAGES IN THIS CHAPTER:

- Your positioning is the essence of your brand in one or two words.

- The positioning will steer your team in the right direction.

- Everything we create needs to be driven by the positioning.

For thirty years the Seawise Giant sailed the oceans, famous for being the longest ship ever built – at 458 m it was longer than the height of the Empire State Building. It could also carry more than any other ship in the world – its dead-weight tonnage a staggering 657,019 tonnes; that's more than all the jumbo jets ever built! It had also come back from the dead; having been sunk during the Iran-Iraq war of 1981, it was later salvaged, repaired and, possibly in recognition of its new lease of life, rechristened Happy Giant.[27]

Despite all its record-breaking stats it's the rudder that's the most interesting because weighing in at a sprightly 230 tonnes,[28] it was one of the smallest elements of the ship but one that had the greatest influence. Without it, that mighty ship would have been directionless. And for me as a brand strategist, my absolute priority when developing recommendations for clients is to get the positioning right because just like a rudder, although it's small in relation to the whole strategy, the influence of the positioning is enormous because it ensures the brand has direction.

The role of brand positioning is to define how the brand is positioned in the minds of the team responsible for delivering it – defining in effect the essence of the organization – and to express in one or two words what makes it tick, what makes the brand unique.

In this chapter we are going to explore why it's so important to define what that brand positioning is. In chapter 1 we talked about the brand strategy acting like the DNA of the brand, and the positioning is the most important element of that DNA – everything we create needs to be driven by the positioning. We will look at how you can generate the one or two words that capture the brand positioning, who will use it and what its role will be. Along the way, we will reference three clients' work as well as take a deep look at how the positioning solved a vexing problem for an international tea brand.

Capturing the positioning in a word or two

Here's a quick exercise. Using only one word, sum up the following brands: Volvo, Amazon and LinkedIn. I'm not suggesting you will know exactly what each one stands for but you'll have an idea. Done it? For me, Volvo means safety, Amazon is convenience and LinkedIn means connections.

> *"Brand positioning lies at the heart of a brand, and what you see on the surface is an expression of that heart."*

However, a quick glance at the advertising and website for Volvo does not reveal any headlines about safety, nor can I find convenience written large on the Amazon site or connections on LinkedIn. I would not expect to either, because the brand positioning lies at the heart of a brand, and what you see on the surface is an expression of that heart. So you would not have seen the rudder that steered the mighty Happy Giant but you saw the course it was taking. It's the very same with the brand positioning; as a customer you see the direction the brand is being taken by how the brand behaves, what it delivers and how it communicates with you, all of which will be directed, to some degree, by the brand positioning.

Here's an example of capturing the essence of a brand from a client I worked with in Germany. Blue Yonder is a leading provider of artificial intelligence solutions to the retail sector. Unlike most of their competitors, the firm does not offer a dashboard or suite of tools to help clients make better decisions, no, they simply use their expertise to deliver the decisions to the client. And in their view, those decisions are the best they can be. Their founder, Prof. Dr Michael Feindt also has strong views about insights, namely that they are overrated – why deliver an insight when you can deliver a decision, he asks. So the idea and power of decisions very much informed the positioning of their brand.

However, we needed to yoke the delivery of decisions to the quality of those decisions and the role those decisions played for clients. In this respect, Blue Yonder saw themselves as leaders, both in the market and in their capacity to guide their clients. From this came the positioning "leading decisions", which distilled the essence of their brand into two words, and whilst it did not appear in any external communications, it drove the direction for the development of the brand going forward.

Hang on though, if it's not going to be expressed externally what exactly is the point of a brand positioning?

For Blue Yonder, their approach to clients was very particular to them, it was also very different from the perceived wisdom about how the market tended to serve clients. They zigged while the world zagged. This recognition, encapsulated in the "leading decisions" positioning, both directed the subsequent brand rollout and, importantly, told the team that the brand strategy "got them".

This explanation ended up in the Brand Guidelines – a sort of design manual for sharing the brand with the communications team and all the agencies charged with producing materials. It also ended up in the Brand Boilerplate – a Word document for the whole organization that contained an explanation of the strategy, key messaging, product descriptions and other guidance that ensured the brand strategy was clearly communicated and easily accessed. (We will look at this more closely in the messaging chapter.)

The brand strategy's number one customer is the team responsible for delivering it and they need to know that it has been developed from the most significant truth about the organization. That truth might not be expressed word for word externally, but it will be known internally. So the brand positioning acts as a reassurance that the brand strategy has been born from truth, that it is authentic, "it is us".

Steering the business to get to the right destination

With a one- or two-word brand positioning, you can make sure the team know the course the brand is taking. It can be used as an internal benchmark to measure any brand strategy activity against that brand positioning – for example, does this message/planned activity/new visual reflect our positioning? The client I mentioned just now was able to sense-check its communications work against its "leading decisions" positioning by gauging how well it was using the idea of decisions in its writing and graphics. It also ensured the brand was far more strident and visible in its sector by increasing the volume of activity to support its leadership credentials.

Here's a great example of positioning for Open Credo, a software consultancy whose whole ethos was around solving business problems with the best and most appropriate emerging technology. As a member of the open source community, and not wedded to any particular platform, their approach could be described as open, intuitive and pragmatic. In the interviews with the team, I kept being told things like:

"We see what others don't."

"We always step back from the immediate to look at the destination."

"When you are on the frontier you need to keep learning."

The essence of Open Credo centered on how they saw the world, their confidence in being able to tailor any solution to any client, so it was not a stretch to land on "clarity" as their positioning – clear, coherent, certain, transparent.

For the client, it captured their independent yet informed point of view and their commitment to applying the maxim that honesty, however awkward that might be, is the best policy. It also drew on the need to recognize some of their internal challenges around growth and to encourage a culture of sharing information with each other. So the brand positioning both reflected the culture of the organization and added to it.

The brand positioning went on to steer the language used to express their value – clarity of thought, clarity of process, clarity of engagement, etc. It also could direct the visual and written expressions of the brand, ensuring the customer always had an uncluttered, crystal-clear view of their offer.

So, when it is authentic, when it resonates with the culture, when it is distinctive and compelling, the brand positioning is a great creative catalyst for developing the direction and expression of the brand. In the Brand Arrow sections over the coming chapters, we will explore how you can define your positioning – it's there, it just needs to be found!

Why less is so much more than more in brand strategy

It's my experience that you should aim to communicate the positioning of a brand quickly and easily. That's why it's so powerful when you do the hard yards to get to those one or two words – they will pack a real punch!

Throughout the book, you will notice that I often ask for a single thing, a sentence, a word, or if I'm feeling generous, three or maybe five bullet points.

"The more you can reduce your word count, the more concentrated the power of the words will become."

Reducing the number of words is a very useful exercise for a number of reasons. Just like reducing a sauce, the more you do it, the more concentrated and flavorsome it becomes, and so the more you can reduce your word count, the more concentrated the power of the words will become.

One of the reasons it becomes more powerful is that you have to make choices; if I only have a few words to sum up the benefits of a product I'll have to do some hard work and prioritize what the most important benefits are – or even the single most important benefit. I'm in good company by the way, Maurice Saatchi, who along with his brother built two of the world's most successful ad agencies, has long since extoled the virtues of a single word to sum up a brand, citing that with attention spans at an all-time low, only one word has a chance of being noticed.[29]

As well as focusing on reducing the number of words, it is essential to place them in order of importance. A long list of your product benefits, for example, isn't much use to your customer because there is no sense of hierarchy, and it's also not much use to your team in guiding what to use in sales messaging, for example. On the other hand, a list that is numbered, with the first being the most important, is helpful to the customer, who can clearly see your main focus, and for your team, who can now use that direction to create marketing materials, for example. With clients, I try and limit the number of items on a list to five or six. Any more and I think we can all get a bit lost – I have never found a list of ten items that couldn't be refined and combined into a list of five items!

However, for me, the most important reason for distilling the brand strategy to a few concentrated and powerful words is what I call "anti-choice". In my experience, brand strategies can be overly long, with quite a few elements, diagrams, flow charts and the like. This can sometimes mean your team may not know what to focus on or they simply chose the elements they like the best. Taking away the ability to choose means you know exactly what your team is drawing on and so you stand a greater chance of ensuring the direction will be consistent.

Reducing the word count will also stand you in very good stead when it comes to the business of writing copy. Whether it's for a website, blog, an event stand or a brochure, for the most part, space is as limited as your customers' attention span, so less is definitely more valuable than more!

In my own experience, the requirement to distill something down to its essence is a very healthy thought process and a very healthy exercise for the team to do together. Better to make the choices during the strategic development than when the website is being built.

Case study: It's all about the soil, darling

So, I asked, "what exactly is biodynamic agriculture?"

"It's about harvesting and planting at the right time of year, as the moon rises, that type of thing."

"Biodynamic is an inspiration with an increasing arc of radiance, like the ripples of a pebble thrown into a pond."

"It's the weird and the whacky, very, very niche, but it brings nothing to the customer."

Any clearer? Me neither.

Problem was, those answers were actually from the team responsible for promoting a brand whose sole differentiator was that it used biodynamic tea in its range. Yes, it was very high quality, yes, it was fair trade, and by dint of being biodynamic it was organic, but in a crowded market, you need something that will stand out. And whilst the team had, with biodynamic, a genuine point of difference, they could not find a way of defining exactly what it was and why consumers should care.

For the record, biodynamic agriculture, founded by Rudolph Steiner in the 1920s, is a precursor to today's organic movement. It treats the farm as a single organism, so the plants, livestock, insects, birds and even people are all considered to be different parts of the same thing. Its overriding principle, therefore, is to ensure the wellbeing of all those elements, and in so doing produce a very high standard of crops.

So far so good, but there are aspects to biodynamic that could be seen as a little, well, out there: spraying crops following the astrological cycle, burying manure in cow horns and storing chrysanthemum oil in chests in darkened rooms, for example. We'll come back to that, but first, let me introduce Kiran, Hampstead Tea's founder and passionate advocate of biodynamic. In fact, it was she who convinced the tea plantation to become biodynamic in the first place.

As we went through the process, which admittedly involved drinking large quantities of delicious tea and listening to Kiran's stories from her childhood in Darjeeling, it became increasingly obvious that this inability to define what lay at the center of the business had stifled their progress and creativity. Whilst the packs looked beautiful, the way the brand spoke to customers was overly corporate and not at all like Kiran.

The job, therefore, was to first define the essence of the brand, its positioning, and then to apply that to the problem of communicating what made them different. I spoke at length with Kiran and her team, I researched biodynamic agriculture, but it wasn't until I spoke to Rajah Banerjee, the owner of the Makaibari tea estate where the tea was grown, that I got closer to finding the essence of the brand. When asked to define biodynamic, Rajah simply said: "It's all about the soil, darling" (apparently he calls everybody darling).

My heart skipped a beat because in my research the only thing I found that the scientists agreed on was the soil. You see, the soil in a biodynamic farm will have more nutrients in it, and more nutrients means healthier plants. That led to the insight, "the better the soil, the better the taste", a phrase that captured the benefit to the customer and the reason why it could be claimed. This provided a concise expression of why biodynamic was relevant to the customer and different to the competition. However, whilst this is still central to the brand, it was not itself the brand positioning.

It was the combination of Rajah's insight, Kiran's passion and the scientific evidence that led to capturing the positioning of the brand as "enrichment". And it made a whole lot of sense.

The brand enriches the experience and pleasure customers can expect by offering the highest quality and purest tea, in blends and flavor combinations that are both delightful and unusual. It's enriching the environment through its pioneering of biodynamic agriculture, and enriching the lives of tea pickers by its commitment to be a 100 percent fair trade. It's also enriching the understanding of the tea industry through its championing of organic and biodynamic tea plantations. The business, of course, will be enriched by drawing on all its strengths to deliver an authentic and contemporary brand across its markets and regions.

But most of all, defining enriching as the positioning gave Kiran the permission to personally engage in how the brand expressed itself. It released a sort of joy that by sharing her passion, knowledge and experiences, Kiran was both enriching her own life and the lives of her customers.

If you want proof of Kiran sharing her passion and enriching the customer's experience of tea you need only to pick up a box of Hampstead Tea's Organic Green Leaf Tea and read the pack copy:

> Darjeeling, up in the hills of the Himalayas, is often shrouded in mist, and I think that contributes to the almost mysterious swirl of flavors you can expect from my Green tea. One sip is grassy and fresh, the next is sweet and flowery. A true voyage of discovery in a cup.

> For this Green tea, we hand-pick only two tender leaves and a bud, which we then lightly steam and dry. So, gentle on the leaf, gentle on the environment, and because it's so high in antioxidants, gentle on you too. Rajah, my friend who owns the Makaibari Estate where this tea comes from,

lives by this simple mantra: "The better the soil, the better the taste".

And in this spirit, he created the world's first organic biodynamic tea garden, where the tea pickers, wildlife and tea bushes all live in harmony with each other in an environment free of chemical pesticides. And as I always pay a premium for my tea, the tea pickers can use that extra income to invest in things they need, like child care, tree planting and school computers.

To enjoy my Green tea, infuse one sachet per cup in freshly boiled water for three minutes.

That's the role of a brand positioning, to chart the course of the brand strategy.

BRAND ARROW QUESTIONS

BA7: How would you describe the essence of your organization?

What are your truths? For Blue Yonder it was all about their approach to delivering decisions, for the IT company it was how they saw the world, and for Hampstead Tea it was about enrichment. Have a think, talk to your team and key customers, jot down some words that you feel reflect what lays at the heart of your organization. These words should focus on how you do things and not what those things are. With my own consulting work, I start by asking clients to sum up in a sentence the value of their brand. I then ask them to sum that up in a word or two. I'm always told that it's impossible, but I always get useful insights when those one or two words are expressed.

Once you have done that exercise, you should have around a dozen words. Put them down on a chart, stand back and ask yourself are these words true, do they resonate with your culture, are they distinctive, are they unique? Cross out the ones that don't make the grade and at the end of this you should have one or two words that have the potential to become your brand positioning.

BA8: Does the brand positioning mark you out as different from your key competitors?

Go back to the work you have done with your three key competitors in chapter 2 and consider what their positioning might be. How are they defining the problem and how are they solving it? This can be done quickly – usually the homepage of their website should provide you with all you need to get a sense of their point. How does it compare to yours? If you feel the words on your list of brand positionings are distinct and compelling, then we have a strong foundation to build from. If, however, you feel they are too close to your competitors, go back and explore how you can create a more distinctive brand positioning – better to do this now and not when you have just launched your new website!

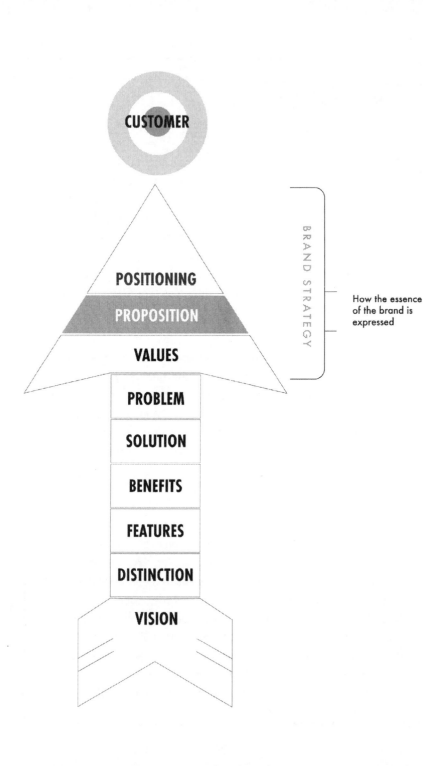

5. BRAND PROPOSITION
Communicating the Essence of the Brand

THE KEY MESSAGES IN THIS CHAPTER:

- The brand proposition is the first few words in the story about to be told.

- It captures the value the brand will deliver.

- It shapes how the brand is expressed to your team and your customers.

Do you remember the beginning of Woody Allen's film *Manhattan*?[30] It opens with moody black and white footage of New York street scenes accompanied by the soaring clarinet solo from Gershwin's "Rhapsody in Blue". The scene is set and the narrator, Woody Allen as Ike, starts to talk about his relationship to the city, but after only a few words, he decides to start again, with a different approach, and then another, with each attempt dismissed as "too corny", or "too preachy", or needing to be more profound, before he finally finds his rhythm, introduces the story and closes with the words, "New York was his town and it always would be". It is quite brilliant, of course very funny, and the absolute opposite of what we should be aiming for with our brand strategy.

The role of the brand strategy is to define and order the key elements of your brand story before you start to communicate them. It is linear – one thing will flow to the next in a way that makes a great deal of sense for the team delivering it and the customers using it. This means that you know your key messaging for your new website, for example, before the design and build starts – so your messaging is driven by you and not by the designer. You know your brand better than anybody and so it is critical that you make the brand messaging crystal clear for your team, for those who are going to create your communications, and of course for your customer.

The brand strategy process, however, is very much an iterative one, with each step having an impact on previous steps. This is why it's a very liberating and edifying experience, because it's a kind of journey of self-discovery for the brand – you get to ask yourself thought-provoking questions and you expect honest answers in return. Your own journey with this book will mean that once you have answered all the questions at the conclusion of each chapter you will have created a pool of knowledge that you will be able to draw on to write your own brand strategy.

I'm saying this now because in this chapter we are going to define a brand proposition, explore its role and take a look at how to construct one. I don't expect you to be able to write your own just yet, because we are too early in the process and you won't know enough about the brand to do so. In fact, I'm not going to ask you to have a go until the very last chapter!

Defining the brand proposition

The reason you need to wait until the end of the book is, frankly, a brand proposition is a challenge to develop because it combines clear strategic thinking with the need for creative flair. It's usually around half a dozen carefully chosen words that capture the promise of the brand in a way that is clear, honest and motivating. It is written for all who have to understand and use the brand, and that starts with you! As the brand owner or creator, you need to be able to succinctly communicate the promise of the brand to the community who need to engage with it. That community will include the team charged with creating products to deliver the brand's services, those who will need to communicate the brand to your customers, your management team (and investors if you have them) who quickly need to be able to grasp what your brand stands for, and of course, the customers who will be buying it!

In effect, it's the start of the narrative of the brand, the first few words of the story about to be told. The brand proposition will shape what your key messages are, and the order in which you share them, which in turn will direct how you construct your communications, which should reflect how your product is delivered and consumed by your customers. Linear!

A good example of a brand proposition is from General Electric, the multi-national conglomerate that's in all kinds of sectors, from healthcare to aviation. Because of the multiplicity of its products the company needed to find a brand proposition that reflected how all those divisions delivered value to its customers. Through a brand strategy process they saw that it was their ability and license to put imagination to work that was really at the heart of everything they did, and so was born the brand proposition "imagination at work".[31] You'll find the line placed just under their logo and appearing across all their corporate communications like the website and press releases.

Another example is from Slack, the work collaboration app used by some of the world's biggest and smallest companies. It lets you message colleagues in your office or on the other side of the world, make video calls and have video conferences, send and store files, in fact, pretty much anything you want to do to be able to work more easily, efficiently and closely with colleagues. Used by over 10 million people in over 150 countries,[32] its brand proposition of "where work happens" redefines the place of work as not a desk or office but an app on your phone or laptop that you carry around with you; in effect, work happens where you happen to be.

Writing a brand proposition

So the best way of writing a brand proposition is to have all you need in front of you before you start. You'll find guidance on the process both in Brand Arrow question 24 and the appendix, but it always helps to have real examples, and here's the first of two recent projects where we have developed a brand proposition.

The client was a design agency and I had been hired to run a Brand Arrow workshop which would deliver a brand strategy in a day – please have a look at my website if that piques your interest! A few days before we met, the team received a primer from me that contained questions to help get them into the right frame of mind for the workshop – they didn't need to send me the answers but to just consider how they might approach them.

On the day itself we had around a dozen questions to tackle, each of which were answered individually before the team then shared their responses.

We then came up with a set of words that reflected a consensus and by the end of the day we had together written the brand strategy. Just like this book, the brand proposition was the very last thing we tackled and we did so armed with an exciting and ambitious brand vision, along with the three most important and compelling drivers to get to that vision and the most significant barriers that the agency would need to address.

We spent time discussing and agreeing the single biggest need that all their clients shared and then defined a sentence that expressed how they met that need. We then identified five key benefits that a client could expect to get from the agency along with the features of their service – in effect, "why hire us" and "how we deliver". After sense-checking those against their competition to make sure they were distinctive, we defined five key messages that are now shaping their marketing. We then looked at their key target customers and, having defined their primary and secondary audiences, agreed the five characteristics they all shared.

All this gave us a platform to have an informed discussion about what really made the agency tick. We agreed a set of values, we defined their brand positioning and then finally got to the brand proposition. All through that day, two themes kept recurring. The first was around how the agency functioned, with every team headed up by a designer who worked in partnership with the client. This meant no layers of bureaucracy to wade through and no precious "prima donnas" to navigate around (the whole team, by the way, were super talented but very down to earth). The second was the recognition of their responsibility to deliver on a business imperative – namely that their clients had to have an impact, to be able to cut through the noise to reach and hold the attention of their customers. Because without that, there would be no business.

From this we came to the brand proposition of "Collaborative Design. Engaged Customers". This spoke to the approach they took to working with clients and the results that approach delivered. It felt like a natural next step, fuelled by the truth that we had unearthed in the workshop, that had been itself collaborative, but also very directional. This is now shaping not only what they communicate but is also how they communicate – their look and feel, new identity, website and marketing materials.

So yes, it's a compelling way to define a brand's promise to customers which can, much like a slogan, appear on marketing materials, but unlike a slogan, the brand proposition's role is to shape how the brand communicates to all its stakeholders, not just its customers.

> *"The brand proposition's role is to shape how the brand communicates to all its stakeholders, not just its customers."*

The anatomy of a brand proposition

The other recent brand proposition example comes from an assignment with Neota Logic, an expertise automation company. It has pioneered a powerful AI-driven software platform that helps customers capture their expertise in a form that can be easily and affordably accessed by all who need that expertise. Its vision centered on ensuring that access to professional expertise could be as affordable and available for as many people as possible, in effect, to democratize access to expertise and in so doing help billions make better decisions. Yes, billions. It's a big vision! The brand proposition formed a critical part in the story of how Neota could move toward that ambitious vision by giving all its stakeholders a glimpse of that vision and in so doing capturing what made the brand relevant to its clients and different from its competitors.

Its brand proposition, "liberating expertise through AI automation", delivered the why (liberating expertise) and the how (AI automation). We choose the word liberate because it's an extremely evocative word, one that is rooted in the ambition expressed in Neota's vision. Experts are few and far between, hard to find and their time limited. For Neota's customers, liberating expertise meant ensuring access to that expertise could be as wide as needed and without the burden of tapping into scarce human or financial resources. The "how" of liberating expertise was achieved through its AI automation software that delivered a deep and wide set of tools yet still enabled its automation applications to be built by customers themselves – without the need to engage time-consuming and costly programmers to do it.

This brand proposition delivered a logical framework that began with the benefit and finished with the process. It was the starting point for the narrative of the brand, in effect, a map for the team to begin to head toward its vision, and a guide for all at the company to be able to present the essence of the brand consistently

> *"Your brand needs to deliver clarity but that does not mean you have to reduce your message to its lowest common denominator."*

and cohesively. It's worth pointing out here that this particular client was in a relatively complex sector with a relatively complex service. This is in fact normal because most clients and most sectors are complex. But let's not think the role of the brand proposition is necessarily to simplify a message, your brand needs to deliver clarity but that does not mean you have to reduce your message to its lowest common denominator. So beware of the temptation to try and simplify because you can often lose the richness, interest and distinctiveness of a brand when you simplify what it stands for. Simplifying a brand message is almost like spoon-feeding customers baby food instead of accepting your customer has the wit and intelligence to consume a full-course meal. You want to employ the intelligence of your customer because that process delivers "skin in the game" – the customer feels engaged with your brand and is more likely to feel attached to it, to have a sense of ownership. The key to a customer wanting to engage with your brand is to make sure it is presented as relevant to their needs. If it's relevant they are much more likely to engage with it regardless of how complex the message is.

Brand proposition vs a slogan

So far in this chapter we have been exploring the brand proposition, and you may well have been thinking, hmm, they look a lot like slogans. Good point. So here is how I distinguish between the two. A slogan, sometimes referred to as a strapline or a tagline, uses a few carefully chosen words written predominantly to appear in marketing campaigns. Based on the brand proposition, the slogan will use a form of words that will appeal primarily to customers – usually placed after the message has been communicated (so at the end of the commercial or at the bottom of a print ad).

The brand proposition is written for both the customer *and* the internal audience. Its role is far greater as it shapes not only what the brand communicates to its customers but what the brand communicates to the team charged with creating and delivering the brand.

Let me give you an example of how the two can work together. Founded in the late 19th century, the *Financial Times* (the *FT*, as it is often referred to)[33] has grown in circulation and stature to become essential reading for the world's most senior financial decision makers. Of all the financial papers, the *FT* is not only the most read it is also viewed as the most credible – its authority, integrity and reach is unquestionable and unrivalled. It would be unthinkable not to seek the views of the *FT* in your role as a senior decision maker in business. And so, given the enormous influence it exerts, I would imagine the brand proposition would be something along the lines of "influencing the influencers". Of course, I don't need to guess the *FT's* slogan, which for decades was "No FT, no comment".[34] It was a very clever way of expressing the influence that the *FT* yields in the world of business by yoking a commonly used phrase in journalism to communicate the *FT's* complete authority in the business world.

Case study: To share is to Banoush.

I love the scene in a *Seinfeld* episode where George Costanza is grazing at a buffet table under the beady and as yet unnoticed eye of another party guest. Upon popping a chip loaded with dip into his mouth the guest squares up to tell him that he has just "double-dipped" – a term George was unfamiliar with. The guest explained, in an exacerbated and pious tone, that by dipping his chip, taking a bite and then dipping again, it was like "putting your whole mouth" into the dip. "Just take one bite and end it" was the guest's final parting shot. George, nonplussed by this breach in etiquette, continued his double-dipping faux pas, a melee started, and the scene moved on. Very funny indeed!

I played that clip to a client in Zurich who was looking to launch a range of Middle Eastern food products into the Swiss market. It captured a major concern that the client had raised, namely that the Swiss are not used to the idea of sitting down to a meal with a table covered in multiple dishes that are intended to be shared. Leaning over each other, tearing off a chunk of pitta to scoop up a dollop of hummus or baba ganoush is commonplace on the tables of the Middle East but a world away from the more formal place setting of "you eat what you order". If we were going to launch this new style food range, we had to help the Swiss know how to eat it!

We came to the idea that the essence of the brand – called Banoush – was all about sharing. Both a small and profoundly big idea because sharing is fundamental to life. We share culture, faith, tastes, languages, responsibility, time, pain, joy, skills, loves, life, and most importantly for the client, we share food. You could say that without it, we wouldn't have society – and perish the thought of a society without hummus!

Armed with that insight – Banoush is about sharing – we were able to explore how we could take the idea of sharing and build it into the narrative of the brand story, to educate diners about the joy of sharing this new cuisine with one another. We simply treated the brand name as a verb to arrive at "to share is to Banoush". It appeared on the packaging designs and the idea of the brand as a guide was reflected in the pack copy which was light in tone but gave clear instructions how to enjoy the product and what it could be paired with. For example:

> There's a lot of stretching with Banoush. You see, our delicious dips, salads and finger foods are made for sharing, so put them in the center of the table and use pitta bread, crisps or crunchy vegetables to scoop up and enjoy. Make sure though you do it with friends because to share is to Banoush.

The sharing proposition also opened up a world of possibilities for the client, as the brand could share with customers food ranges like tapas from Spain or street food from India that would be true to its role and would expand the client's horizons from a focus on Middle Eastern food to a focus on bringing "sharing" food from around the world to the tables of Swiss diners.

BRAND ARROW QUESTIONS

BA9: What is your customer's greatest need?

What is it you do for your customers? What is the problem that you are solving? This may seem like an easy question, but it isn't, because your customers may have lots of needs – or their needs may differ from one to the next. For this exercise, we need to define an overarching need because we are then going to focus on creating a brand that responds to that need. So, make a note of all of the needs using one sentence for each and then put them into an order with the most pressing need at the top of the list.

BA10: How do you meet that need?

Now that you have defined your customer's most pressing need, describe how you are able to meet that need. Once you have done that, it will be useful to go down your list of needs and define your solutions for each one as this can be used later in the process. Remember though, it needs to be distinctive from others in the same sector and should stem from the work you have done in defining your positioning. Once you are done, you should have two sentences that capture the problem you are solving and how you plan to solve it. We will come back to these when we develop the brand messaging in chapter 10.

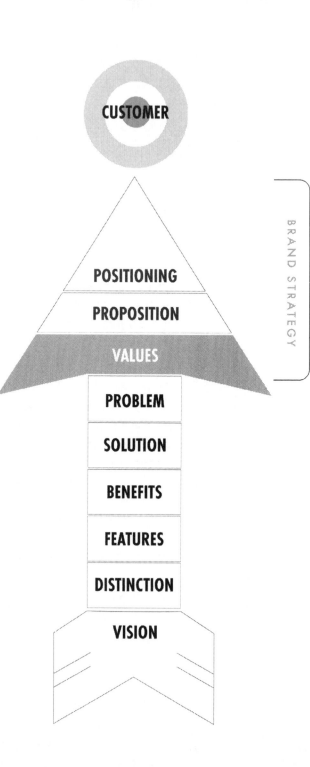

6. VALUES
Capturing the Character of the Brand

THE KEY MESSAGES IN THIS CHAPTER:

- Values define your brand's character, behavior and attitude.

- They express how the customer should experience your brand.

- Values are the benchmark you and your customer will use to judge your brand.

It is said that the values of the IKEA brand – togetherness, simplicity, respect and cost consciousness – are in fact the values of Älmhult, the birthplace of its founder Ingvar Kamprad. Älmhult is also the first place in the world to have an IKEA store,[35] and at the time of writing, Manhattan the last. In between, there have been some 422 stores opened in 50 countries,[36] and those values have played a fundamental role in shaping the brand and helping IKEA become the world's biggest furniture maker.[37] Let's take a look at the value of cost consciousness; on the surface, not that exciting a value, until you look a little deeper and see how fundamental it has been in shaping the brand.

If you have ever shopped at one of their stores, you know for the larger items you'll need to go and grab a trolley and load up your flat-packed furniture yourself – and this, of course, means you do the work that would normally be done by an employee, and so this delivers a saving that is reflected in the cost of the item. It also means that a great deal of IKEA's products can fit in a customer's car and so avoid the need to pay delivery charges.

The whole idea of flat-packed furniture was popularized by Gillis Lundgren, a catalogue manager for the firm who, in the early days of IKEA, when tasked with taking a table to a photo shoot, had to take the legs off to get it into the back of his car.[38] This got him thinking about how much easier it would be to ship their products if everything was flat-packed. Not only would it substantially reduce transportation costs, it would also reduce the labor costs as much of the assembly would be done by the customer and not the employee. A great deal of these savings could then be passed onto the customer, thus helping to fulfill his bosses' ambition to make good furniture available to the masses.

This commitment to cost consciousness shaped how IKEA expanded and is very present in today's IKEA. Its furniture uses as many common parts as it can and it limits the number of significant design changes in each range to ensure it can use many of the same processes and materials to manufacture them. Since the start of the century, it has pioneered a process where solid wood can be replaced with hollow wood. Take for example table legs, many of which are now hollow and filled with a cardboard honeycomb that delivers strength, reduces the amount of wood required to make the item and so reduces its weight and its cost.[39] IKEA's drive for cost reduction is also closely aligned to its wholehearted commitment to the environment – which reflects another of its values, that of respect. By embedding the value of cost consciousness into all its business practices, tied to its vast scale, it means that IKEA's customers can expect to buy furniture that is remarkably good and remarkably inexpensive.

So, IKEA's values are influential, they shape how the brand is developed and how it is experienced by customers. In this chapter, we will define the role of values, and look at examples of brands that use their values to deliver a cohesive experience for customers, and others that use values to differentiate themselves in the market.

What are brand values?

"Do you have company values?" I once asked a client. "Yes," I was told, "you'll find them in the kitchen." Turns out this particular company had six kitchens and to this day I don't know in which kitchen they were kept! Of course, you can't keep values in kitchen cupboards because it's not possible to interact with other humans without displaying values. If meetings always start on time that says something of the values of the place, if they rarely do, that says something else. When I discuss values with clients it's often in the context of the need to capture what's in the ether, in the fabric of the place, because the environment in which we work will reflect how we all behave – for good or bad. Most of the time it's good, but if it's not defined then it will keep evolving, and so what employee

"If you can't express your values, you can't use them."

number 3 thinks of the values of the workplace may be different from employee number 30. So, there is a need to legislate the values, to define them and write them down, because values play a vital role in how the brand is developed. If you can't express your values, you can't use them.

Earlier in the book, we looked at how a brand is valued, and a brand's values are a fundamental part of that process because of the influence they exert over the brand. So, brand values describe the character of an organization – how it behaves, how it treats its staff, the tone it uses in communications, how it presents itself to the world, and the products or services that it produces. Mike Coupe, the CEO of Sainsbury's, sums up the role of values brilliantly:[40]

> Our values are the thread running through every part of our business. Whether it's making it easier to choose healthier products, or saving money and reducing food waste at home – we're always looking for ways to make life better for our customers while also doing the right thing for our colleagues, shareholders, the planet and society.

Values play a vital role in keeping you and your customers focused on what your brand stands for. For your team, brand values can be used both as a source of inspiration and guidance when developing new brand related initiatives. They also enable the team to sense-check whether their resulting work reflects the brand values. For your customers, brand values help them recognize your brand, reinforce the relationship they have with it and, critically, act as a benchmark for the brand to live up to. Six values are enough to provide a great sense of the character of the brand but not too many that people glaze over. It's also important to provide a sentence after each value to define exactly what each one means as this helps those charged with delivering the brand to really get to know its character (this might be the team creating a new product, a design agency developing a corporate brochure or the sales team putting together a pitch).

Here's an example of a selection of values developed for a data analytics provider in the healthcare sector, along with some notes from me on why each value was chosen.

Independent – a credible and critical friend, trusted to stand as part of, and apart from, the health sector. (It was important for the brand to be seen as an independent voice but still very much engaged in the sector.)

Connected – collaborative and cohesive in development, relevant and accessible in delivery. (The healthcare sector is incredibly complex and often disjointed, so the brand needed to communicate its ability to make the right connections.)

Specialist – a deep knowledge of customer needs, coupled with a unique application of clinical acumen. (A key differentiator in the market, and an acknowledgment that delivery of services requires a depth of expertise and the ability to apply that expertise in the most relevant ways for a variety of roles.)

So, you can see how each value is directive, and each has a strategic role to play in shaping how the brand is presented. What we don't want to do is waste this chance to define the brand by citing generic values like honesty and professionalism; clearly they are important, but you would expect both to be a matter of course for any organization. So, values are a platform to communicate the best things about the organization, but they can also be used as a way of dealing with the worst things too, or at least, acknowledging a problem and defining a means of dealing with it.

Here's an example: I worked with a client whose base of operations could not have been further apart – organizing a conference call meant that at least one party would either have to stay up very late or get up with the sparrows! One of the repercussions was the regions were not always in synch. Part of the narrative of one value was around vision and the need to first express that vision and then to "share progress toward that vision with the team and clients on a regular basis". This is an antidote value, one that acknowledges there is a problem and provides a commitment to address it.

Of course, writing down a set of values does not make them valuable. The value comes when they are put to work in driving how the brand is experienced.

Values bring your brand together

Let's look at a brand that has been able to consistently deliver its values to bind the experience of its brand, not only across different products, markets and regions, but without wholly owning many of the companies that use its brand. That brand is Virgin. Started by Sir Richard Branson as a record label in the 1970s, it has grown to be one of the world's most iconic brands, often tearing up the rule book about what a brand can and can't do. There are over 40 Virgin-branded companies across the world[41] running a mind-boggling diversity of services including airlines, banks, mobile networks, gyms, trains, healthcare and even space travel. There are many reasons why Virgin is able to do this successfully, and one of the most important reasons is its focus on brand values to frame a set of customer expectations across its varied portfolio.

Virgin refers to its values as the brand's backbone and lists them as follows: "providing heartfelt service, being delightfully surprising, red hot and straight up, while maintaining an insatiable curiosity and creating smart disruption."[42] Let's have a whistle-stop tour of how customers are being treated to Virgin's heartfelt service.

Virgin Money (the bank, established in 2000 after the collapse of Northern Rock) offers its members free access to one of eight city center lounges, where they can relax in comfortable surroundings, read a paper, take a meeting, and enjoy free refreshments and Wi-Fi access.[43] Virgin Holidays builds customer excitement around their booked holiday by using travel experts to recommend excursions and events that are tailor made for each customer.[44] Virgin Trains has recently partnered with Amazon's Alexa to enable customers to buy train tickets simply by using their voice.[45] And let's not forget one of Virgin's most iconic companies, Virgin Atlantic, which offers to pick up business passengers in a limo and introduced the first individual in-flight entertainment system back in 1989![46]

So, of course, we can look at a brand, as we have done, and single out how a value is expressed, but it's when they work together that the role of brand values is truly elevated. Back to IKEA, and its value of cost consciousness is informed by its value of respect – this ensures that driving out cost will not be at the expense of the quality of its products, the quality of the lives of its staff and suppliers and, of course, the quality of the environment. The value of simplicity, expressed in its clean and uncluttered designs, allows the manufacturing processes to be streamlined, and finally, its value of togetherness has become the hallmark of how the teams in the stores and at HQ collaborate with each other.

> *"Ignore your values at your peril because you will be judged on them."*

Finally, a sober word of warning. If your claimed values are ignored or even abused, your brand can be torn apart. We all know VW is famed the world over for its value of reliability – look down any street and you'll find all ages of its models still going strong. This value has been severely compromised by the recent revelation in the US that it installed software in over half a million of its diesel cars that falsified emissions data. The company has since been fined billions, executives are serving jail sentences and the scandal continues to play out.[47] That's a pretty catastrophic example, but the principle is the same: ignore your values at your peril because you will be judged on them.

Values can mark you out as different

Mario Schlosser and his wife, going through their first pregnancy, were bewildered by the seemingly needless layers of complexity the US health insurance process demanded and their powerlessness over their choice of healthcare provider. That same year Mario founded Oscar Health Insurance to provide a people-friendly health insurance company that would, above all things, connect to the customer. Oscar (the name was chosen to engage with members on a human level) used technology to take out complexity, the endless forms and the impenetrable jargon usually associated with health insurance.[48]

Oscar assigns a team of five health insurance guides and a healthcare professional to lead each member through that complexity to the right solution. It is called the concierge team, deliberately steering away from health insurance jargon to one that focused on service (remember its the concierge in the hotel lobby you go to for help and guidance). Every time a need arises, the member calls and gets the same team, and this builds up a personal connection to the brand. Oscar also provides an app that gives members the ability to speak to a doctor within fifteen minutes, at any time, on any day, with over 90 percent of these calls resulting in the issues being resolved. Both these services mark the brand out as different from their bigger and long-established competitors by delivering a connected, more personal service.[49]

Here's another example, on a subject close to most people's hearts – chocolate. Only a few years ago the British high street was not the place for a chocolate lover. Customers had to choose between cheap chocolate bars sold in general stores, a specialist chain with a rich heritage but an unexciting range, or super expensive providers that were out of reach for all but the most avid connoisseur. This is a problem for a country that consumes on average over 180 chocolate bars per person a year![50] In 2004, Angus Thirlwell and Peter Harris changed all that by launching Hotel Chocolat on the values of authenticity, originality and ethics.[51]

The entrepreneurs started by making sure the amount of sugar in their chocolate decreased and the amount of cocoa increased – sugar is cheaper than cocoa and many milk chocolate bars have as much as twice the amount of sugar to cocoa. Two years later the pair bought a cocoa plantation in Saint Lucia that enabled the brand to truly become an expert in every part of cocoa cultivation and production. The brand was able to leverage the passionate members of its Chocolate Club, which launched in 1998 and is made up of thousands of "chocoholics" who provide an expert sounding-board for the brand.[52]

What makes Hotel Chocolat so successful is aligning that authenticity to its originality. For example, instead of producing the traditional chocolate bar with its 'break off' squares, the brand offers customers a single slab of chocolate with all kinds of exotic combinations like pistachio and honey or banoffee pie. Even calling itself a hotel is original, although ironically, as well as over 100 stores, it does own a hotel, cafes, restaurants and a school of chocolate. At the same time, Hotel Chocolat ensures the cocoa, the prized ingredient the brand is built on, is ethically sourced by creating its own program to engage with the cocoa farmers across a range of subjects like fair pay, women's empowerment, education and stable trading.[53]

The brand's foundation was and still is based on authenticity, originality and ethics, and these three values have marked Hotel Chocolat out as very different from what the high street offers, much to the delight of the British chocolate lover!

Case study: The Champion

After an hour, I had gone through the findings from all my interviews, captured the results of the workshop and crystallized it all in a set of brand strategy recommendations. I was exhausted, happy that I had given the assignment my all, but then dismayed as I watched the client, without a word, leave the room.

This was not normal. But then again, nor was the client.

For the last 25 years, Dean Cycon, founder of Dean's Beans, had been using coffee as a vehicle for change to deliver a real and lasting difference to small farming communities across the globe. Dean's razor-sharp mind and deep commitment to the plight of some of the world's most marginalized communities had lit up the lives of coffee growers and drinkers the world over.

Put simply, Dean is one of the most remarkable people you will ever come across! However, Dean does not follow the crowd, and by definition nor did his coffee brand and so, early on in the assignment, it became apparent that if I was to get to know the brand I would have to get to know the man. The values of the brand were in effect the values of Dean and so my role was to get under his skin to put some order to how the brand's values were expressed. The first value came at me like a stampede of wild horses – his charisma. His presence and sheer energy could fill a room full of people in a heartbeat, and in that room he could hold each individual's attention as if it was just the two of them. A gift it may be, but at its root is a heartfelt passion for the underdog, care for other people, and a granite-like belief that it's the right thing to do.

He was a radical. Dean's innovation and inquisitive intuition came from fresh thinking, not burdened by "the way we do things here". It's a simplicity of thought that always goes to the heart of the matter, by more often than not listening to the people most important to Dean – the coffee farmers. He believed traditional development practices boxed in the farmers' thinking by maintaining the belief that change only comes from the outside, creating a reliance on others with no sense of ownership. He coined the phrase People Centered Development to describe a paradigm shift he wanted to deliver – to open the box to a world of possibilities.

That radical value came from another of his values, that of being connected to the farmers. He believed it was the communities themselves that knew what was needed, and not the aid organizations or governments. Dean would always spend time with the farmers, and by seeing with his own eyes and listening to the communities he used his expertise to steer a "solution" to a "problem".

But there was a significant issue. Dean was tired. Because of the incredible energy that he put into the business and because it was all on his shoulders, he was running low. Through the process I had seen this and had been intentional about using the brand strategy as a way of attempting to rekindle the spark that had lit up the coffee world for so long. At the core of my recommendations was the brand positioning of 'champion'. This reflected Dean's passion to champion the cause of small farmers, to be a champion for young people, showing them how they could affect real change, and of course, a champion for a decent cup of joe! His passion, as displayed in his values, was to open the eyes of farmers to their own potential, and open the minds of consumers to a better cup of coffee.

After a what seemed like an eternity, Dean came back to the meeting room, tears rolling down his cheeks, a huge smile splashed across his face, and told me our work together had reignited his passion for the brand and that was, in his words, more valuable than gold.

BRAND ARROW QUESTIONS

BA11: Define the values that sum up the character of your organization.

Spend some time exploring what things go really well in your organization, and try to capture the reasons you think they do. Have a look at your products and services and make a note of the values they embody. Very importantly, look also at what doesn't work so well and ask yourself what values you would need to adopt to deal with those issues. If it's just you, ask the people you deal with – customers and suppliers, for example. Look at your materials and ask yourself what values they are projecting. If there's more than one of you, ask the team; perhaps make it a confidential email or an anonymous suggestion box.

BA12: Choose six values and write a sentence that expresses exactly what you mean by each.

You will end up with a lot more than six values, and so look at clustering the responses into themes and then name the themes. For example, if there are a lot of responses around speed of delivery, fast response to customer queries, efficiencies in internal systems, you might cluster these round the word effectiveness. These will become your six values. Use the words in each cluster to write a sentence about each value to give a deeper sense of what that value stands for. This is important because it takes away any guesswork about the specific use of each value, it provides a very useful start for writing copy for marketing and sales, and it acknowledges that some values are a work in progress or even a response to an issue that has come up in the process.

7. NAME
A Wide Open Door to Your Organization

THE KEY MESSAGES IN THIS CHAPTER:

- You can't share your brand without sharing your brand's name.

- A good name is an open door to your business.

- A bad name means that door is closed.

Carl's Hill. It's a famous beer. Have you heard of it? It was founded back in the 19th century by Jacob Jacobson. A collector of art, a passionate believer in science and a successful businessman, Jacob decided it was time to put all three of his passions to work and brew the perfect beer. So he bought a hill, built his brewery on top of it and, casting out for a name, decided to call the beer after his son Carl. And as it was on a hill he brought the two words together to form the name Carl's Hill.[54] But of course, the hill was in Denmark and so it was a berg, and hence the name Carlsberg was born. Fast forward to this century and it's a testament to the power of that name that when the brewer recently changed every aspect of the brand – from its formulation to its packaging – the name stayed.[55]

However, quite often when organizations change, grow and evolve, what seemed like a good idea at the time of the launch can sometimes be light years away from where the company is ten years on. In this chapter, we are going to explore how to understand whether you have a good, bad or ugly brand name and the kind of actions needed to maximize the impact of a good one or remedy the problems of a bad one. We are also going to look at three different types of brand names:

- Transactional – names that are created based on the product or its benefits.

- Transformational – names that evoke a benefit or try to capture the values of the brand.

- Traditional – names that didn't go through any sort of brand strategy process, but are usually the name of the founder or founders and have since become part of our culture.

However the name turns out, it's a big deal and so needs to be treated carefully as changing a name means replacing all the materials with the old name and time and financial costs in communicating the name change. That said, if it's change that is being communicated, then changing the name of the brand is the biggest signal that can be made!

The good, the bad and the ugly

If you don't let your brand grow with your business, or encourage it to adapt to changing tastes and keep it in touch with your culture, it ends up being something your customers have to navigate around. Your brand is a big open door into your business. The role of a brand name is to make

> *"Your brand is a big open door into your business. The role of a brand name is to make that door as wide as possible."*

that door as wide as possible so that customers can see clearly what your organization has to offer. Good brand names can do this and will help enormously in telling your story. Of course, on its own it won't sell a thing but a brand name that captures the value you deliver will be enormously helpful in making a sale more likely. Let's look at a good one.

Google has a nine-year-old boy to thank for the origins of its brand name. Back in 1920, the young Milton Sirotta told his uncle (an American mathematician by the name of Edward Kasner) that a good name for a very, very, very big number would be googol. He agreed, and over time googol became the commonly accepted term to describe a number that is equal to 1 followed by 100 zeroes. Fast forward to 1997, and the story goes that a young company named BackRub (a nod to their work in analyzing the backlinks of the web) were brainstorming a new name, and its founder, Larry Page, liked Googol as it alluded to the huge amount of data available to be searched online.[56] However, and somewhat ironically for a search engine company, the name Google and not Googol was mistakenly checked and

Google.com was presented to the founders.[57] Despite the error, it was liked and so the name stood. It has, of course, become an extremely successful brand name, even entering the *Oxford English Dictionary* in the June 2016 edition as the verb used to denote using the Google search engine to find information on the Internet.[58] If you don't believe me, you can google it!

A good name is an asset that needs to be used, so make sure you have your brand name front and center of all you do. A bad name though is a liability; it actively pulls against the brand strategy, taking customers away from the intended direction of the brand. It's like placing a huge granite boulder in front of the door to your business and making customers squeeze past it to get to you, or worse and more likely, they fail to notice you in the first place. If you do have a bad name, then a brand strategy can help you deal with it. Here's a story from a recent project with a PR agency who, by the founder's admission, had a "bad 'un".

The agency worked across a number of sectors, but the core business and most of the value came from delivering services to the construction sector. Its founder, having started life as a journalist for a number of construction magazines, knew the sector backward and was very well connected within it. Together we identified a 'sweet spot' of clients that, with a market share below the top three, were too small for the big specialist agencies but too big for the small generalist agencies. From this, we came to a brand proposition around delivering clients big agency specialist expertise but at the price of the smaller generalist agencies. This drove the development of a new brand strategy that formalized this approach and whose focus was solely on the construction sector. The only problem left to deal with was its brand name. For good reasons (now long forgotten) the founder had used the name of a particular type of operatic music to christen the PR agency. Unfortunately, the name was hard to pronounce correctly, hard to spell and most importantly, a great distance from the construction sector. The brand strategy process helped create a new name for the agency that both reflected the sector and amplified its credentials – and we will come to how we can create brands names shortly.

There's a third category, and I feel very mean calling it ugly, but as a homage to Clint Eastwood's spaghetti western classic, I think it's a

> *"A bad name is a liability; actively taking customers away from the intended direction of the brand."*

price worth paying. Ugly, or indifferent, names are ones that are neutral, not really damaging the brand but not supporting it either. This type of name needs to be helped along because your name is the most widely used part of your brand. It's the first word in the story of your brand, it will be the most spoken – "I work for", "have you heard of", "can I have" – and it will be the most widely presented – on business cards, social media, websites and products. So it has to work for you because it's everywhere!

I have a client who for the last 30 years has provided concise, accurate and readily accessible guidance on every aspect of pensions legislation. The industry-leading service is seen as vital in supporting its members in the complex and seemingly forever changing regulatory environment of UK pensions. It has a tremendous reputation for combining a deep knowledge of pensions with a keen sensitivity to the practical needs of its customers. Its brand name is Aries, coined after the initials of its first research project, which very neatly spelt the word Aries. The name was known, but beyond that it did not give a hint of the value of the service it provided.

A few years back we worked together to develop a brand strategy, and we recognized that the essence of the brand revolved around its ability to deliver insight on every aspect of pensions legislation and to then provide guidance on how best to apply that insight in the customers' own delivery of services. We took this brand positioning of 'applied insight' and shaped a new brand around it, which also included modifying the brand name from an unspecific but well known "Aries" to a directional and still well known "Aries Insight". This helped the brand story get started from the first word, shaped the new marketing and sales materials, enabled the team to reinforce its value to current members, and critically, for a brand intent on growing, introduce that value to prospective members.

So how do you know what type of name you have? By "asking it" a number of questions that will help you understand how aligned your brand name is to your brand strategy. Here's the checklist:

- Is the name relevant to your brand positioning?

- Can it be placed before or after the brand proposition?

- Does the name feel in synch with your brand values?

- Does the name lend authority and legitimacy to your vision?

- Is it applicable across all your products or services?

- Does your name reflect the sector you are in?

- Does the name help your customer know what you do?

- Does it communicate your relevance to your customer's needs?

- Does it differentiate you from your competitors?

- Is it easy to pronounce and spell?

If by doing this process you end up answering mostly yes, then your brand name is a good one and the task is therefore to make sure you are using it as effectively as possible. If your answers are predominantly no, then your brand name is fighting against the direction the brand strategy is taking you and it needs to be changed. If you are somewhere in the middle then your name is not pulling its weight and you need to enhance it by adding a further word before or after it or redeveloping your logo so that it clearly describes what your brand purpose it. In Brand Arrow question 14 you will find a process to create a new or enhanced brand name.

What's in a name?

Our names are of course the product of our parent's imagination and not the result of a strategic process – parents don't usually decide the typology of name to give their child. And whilst in business there is a more strategic approach to naming a brand, it's still not an exact science, with names being chosen for a myriad of reasons. These can range from the very strategically grounded (it captured the brand strategy) to reflecting the things that really matter to the founders (it's a mix of the first two letters of our children's first names) to the not grounded at all but it sounded pretty cool. And all that is good. However, if we are to look at creating a new brand name or adapting an existing one, it is helpful to consider the different roles a name can play. Let's look at the three typologies mentioned at the start of this chapter.

The first I call transactional and its role is to:

- identify the purpose of the brand (for example, salesforce.com is a tool that helps all kinds of teams, especially in sales, perform better);[59]

- provide an idea of its functional benefits (PayPal – a trustworthy way of paying for products online);[60]

- allude to the properties of the brand (Coca Cola – named after two of its ingredients, the coca leaves and kola nuts).[61]

Facebook is a popular transactional brand name, it literally does what the name suggests – a "book of faces" on the Internet that allows the user to share news, connect with friends and join communities. From the business world, LinkedIn is another, where the business community can "link" with each other, exchange contact details, create relationships and share content. I like the example of Subway, now the largest fast food chain in the world. It started life in 1965 as "Pete's Super Submarines" as a way of offering a healthier version of fast food (for the non-US readers, a sub is short for submarine, the name often given to a soft baguette-style sandwich). It turns out that their early radio commercials started to cause confusion because "Pete's Super" sounded a lot like "pizza" to listeners and so the name was changed to Pete's Subway, and later to Subway. It has delivered a great platform for the brand to both communicate its core offering of sub sandwiches and provide the customer with the ability to personalize a wide range of bread and fillings "their way".[62]

The second type of name is transformational, names that do not identify a functional benefit, but rather focus on a state of mind that the brand wants to communicate. A good example would be Patagonia. The outdoor clothing brand name evokes the soaring mountains and deep lakes of the

South American region, although most of its customers will never hike the trails of Patagonia. Transformational brand names can also express the emotional benefits the brand can deliver. The Virgin brand name for example speaks to the benefits the brand will deliver even before the customer enters the plane, train, gym, bank, etc.

BT Cellnet, a competitor of the Orange brand I featured in chapter 1, is a good example of a brand moving from a transactional to a transformational name. In 2002, BT Cellnet (a blend of the words cellular and network) rebranded to the name O2.[83] To the chemists it's the chemical symbol for an oxygen molecule, signifying the essential element for life. To the marketers it's positioning the brand's services as an essential element for life, reflecting their large range of value added services and innovations that have marked the brand as different from its competition. The identity and much of the advertising since its launch has consistently used distinctive images of air bubbles seemingly rising up through water. It's been a successful transition, with the brand now the second largest network in the UK.[84]

The key to a good transformational brand name is that the expression and intent of the brand is represented in a way that is authentic. The O2 brand has been successful because it has a clear vision of how its name could drive the development of its story. This was not the case unfortunately with the Post Office who in 2001, having moved from state to private control, decided to change its name to Consignia, to convey the fact the brand did more than just mail deliveries.[85] However, the new management team did not factor in the affection for, and high trust in, the Post Office name and it was not welcomed by the public, who viewed the new name as confusing and meaningless. Consignia was consigned to the bin 16 months and £2m later,[86] and the Post Office brand name was once again a feature of most UK high streets.[87]

The final name typology is what I refer to as traditional, where the brand name is taken from the founder's name. Whilst we are surrounded by many long-established brands named after their founders – Ford, Woolworths, McDonald's and Hilton to name but a few – with the exception of professional services and fashion, it's a practice not commonly used now. If you are in a sector that requires you to develop a founder brand, or you are working with an established founder brand, then make sure the identity, brand proposition and imagery all reflect and are consistent with the brand strategy.

Finally, to end the chapter it's worth acknowledging that strategy can sometimes be muscled out of the room by a forceful character that makes a call and it just clicks. One such example is the name given to a Californian consumer electronics company. The story goes that after a trip to Oregon, a place the founder referred to as an "apple orchard", he recommended the name Apple simply because he loved apples. The founding team, not at all convinced, agreed a 5 p.m. deadline to come up with a better sounding, more technical name. They didn't manage it, the name stuck[68] and it was not the first time Steve Jobs got his own way!

Case study: Keeping the door wide open

In chapter 3 I shared the story of Ten Thousand Villages (USA) and their need to get back on track and how the vision statement played an important role in providing the whole organization with a shared purpose. I'm going to return to this client now to share with you how, back in the early 1990s we had a different problem to solve, and that was the fact that the name had become a barrier for their business.

At the time, the retailer was called Self Help Crafts and they had finally had enough of customers coming into their stores and asking to be better cooks, mechanics, weavers or even better lovers! Since the fair trade retailer launched in the 1940s, the whole self-help movement had been born, and while the staff were delighted with their customers' noble ambitions, it had nothing at all to do with what they actually sold in their stores.

Clearly, the name was getting in the way of their brand and so needed to be changed.

Based in Akron, Pennsylvania, the retail chain collaborates closely with communities in over thirty countries to design and create items that can be sold through their stores in the US. They pay a fair price, provide advance payment, are always in it for the long term and endeavor to ensure every link in their supply chain is as ethical as possible.

However, back to 1995 and their name had evolved from a wide open door and a perfect platform to tell their stories to one that became almost a closed door that needed to be navigated around. The job of the brand strategy was to get that door open again by changing the name to one which was a wide open invitation for customers to come into their stores.

What better place to look for a new name than the communities the organization works with?

Together with the leadership team, we created the new name Ten Thousand Villages, inspired by a quote from Mahatma Gandhi who insisted that the real India was not to be found in the cities but in its thousands of villages. This chimed with where the essence of the brand was and still is – the rural communities where most of the products are made by hand.

This striking name provided the perfect place to start to tell stories, to share the lives of the artisans and to showcase their products, everything from jewelry to textiles to furniture.

The name needed an identity and it seemed a natural step to illustrate its intent by creating an unbroken line tracing the outline of village houses across different cultures, each with their doors and windows open suggesting a willingness to share their stories and products with the world.

But the story does not end there. I was invited back to the US 22 years on to review that work and see if the market and culture had moved on again and so render the work in need of an evolution or even to change it.

I'm glad to say that nothing was broken and so nothing needed to be fixed.

The challenge was more around refreshing how the team thought about and used the brand. You see, it had slipped into being treated as three words and a logo instead of a source of inspiration and direction for the staff, their partners and most of all, their customers.

The answer we came to was to understand that the name and identity describe where all their stuff comes from – and from there we started to build a brand strategy that is embedded in their story. We found the treasure that had been hidden for a while.

BRAND ARROW QUESTIONS

BA13: What's the story of your brand name and is it still relevant today?

Think back to when you started your business or the time you coined the name of your start-up idea. Write a paragraph that states how your name came about. Was it by accident? Did it reflect your ideas for your business? Have those ideas now changed? Once you have done that, run your name through the good, bad, ugly checklist and work out how well your name has done. If the answers are mainly yes, make a list of five measures you can take to ensure your name is more central to your brand story. If the answers are either a mix of yes and no, or just a straight no, head to the next question.

BA14: What new name or enhanced name best reflects your brand strategy?

Your brand strategy, once complete, will provide the catalyst to create or enhance a brand name – it's like a pool of knowledge you can draw from to develop the name. This is the way I generate new names for clients, and it can be done in a workshop or on your own. Take a couple of flip charts and draw a set of columns – around a dozen will be enough. At the top of the first column write the brand positioning (if it's two words, write the second in the second column). Use the six words that define your brand values for the next column and the final four to five columns to capture the keywords from your brand proposition. Once you are done, use a thesaurus to discover new ways of expressing the headings of each of your columns.

continued

You should end up with around a dozen in each column. From that exercise, some words will emerge that could be candidates for the new or enhanced name. Once you have a shortlist, see which ones are available as URLs. Check if the name is already registered and if it is already trademarked and you'll end up with a small number that meet the brand strategy and are available. Take those and see how well each works with your products and services and ask your team and your key customers what their preference is. Once you have decided, ask your lawyer to cross the t's and dot the i's and you'll have your new or enhanced name!

8. LOGO
Expressing the Point of the Brand in an Instant

THE KEY MESSAGES IN THIS CHAPTER:

- Brand strategy delivers design direction.

- Every element of your logo should tell your brand story.

- It's the visual start point of all your marketing communications.

Napoleon Bonaparte is rumored to have said: *"Un bon croquis vaut mieux qu'un long discours"*,[69] or for those of us not fluent in French, "a picture paints a thousand words". When it comes to creating a logo for your brand it's important those thousand words are telling the right story. And that's primarily the job of the brand strategy, to provide direction to the design team in creating a logo or to ensure that any finessing of an existing logo remains true to the intent of the brand.

The logo is not the brand, but a product of the brand strategy and its job is to represent the brand graphically so that whenever the customer sees the logo, they see the brand it represents. The most successful logos can do this without even having to feature the name of the brand – if you have an iPhone, you'll find the apple logo on the reverse and if you have a magnifying glass you may just be able to find the name Apple on it too.

Perhaps on a car journey when it's time for a break you, like me, will have scoured the horizon for a pair of golden arches to let you know there's a McDonald's coming up. Possibly the most famous is the Nike logo, the rounded tick, or swoosh as it's called, seen everywhere from professional sports teams and the shirts of famous sports stars to the millions of us that jog, do Pilates, play golf, etc. The swoosh represents a brand worth over $32bn in 2019, making it the world's most valuable clothing brand.[70]

In this chapter we are going to look at what makes a good logo, how a brand strategy can ensure that it does the best job in representing the brand, and the different mechanisms available to you in getting a logo designed. We will then explore the psychology of shapes and colors and take that knowledge into how you might think about your own logo development.

What's makes a good logo?

Logos are very good at communicating ideas quickly and have been doing that job for a very long time. The oldest recorded logo belongs to the Belgium brewer Stella Artois, which for over 600 years has featured the depiction of a horn on its beer bottles.[71] Twinings Tea, Bass, Levi's, Shell, and Heinz ketchup are all brands that have been using the same logo for over 100 years.[72] So what does it take for a logo to be good?

> *"The logo doesn't have to tell the whole story, but whatever part it tells, it needs to be true."*

Firstly, it needs to be distinctive – to be easily recognizable and stand out from other brands. As an example, and sticking with the Bass logo, you can make out a couple of bottles of Bass beer by their vivid red triangles in Manet's painting of the bar at the Folies-Bergère.[73] And staying with the art theme, Campbell's Soups, with its distinctive white font logo on a red background has been a feature on supermarket shelves for decades, along with Andy Warhol's famous paintings from 1962.[74]

Secondly, the logo needs to be true to the brand it represents. So that means you either need to see elements of the brand strongly represented in the logo or be able to use the logo as a starting point to express those elements. The logo doesn't have to tell the whole story, but whatever part it tells, it needs to be true. When BMW relaunched the Mini brand in 2000 it featured a logo very similar to the logo from Mini's heyday in the 1960s[75] – it did this to reassure customers that the spirit of the brand was the same.

Thirdly, the logo needs to be memorable. We are all aware of the multitude of images we are exposed to on a daily basis, but brand logos have always needed to enter and stay in our minds. Take a look on the back of a pair of Levi's and you'll see a couple of horses pulling a pair of jeans in opposite directions, connoting the toughness of the denim with its unique copper rivets. The story goes that back in the 19th century customers would ask for "those pants with two horses".[76]

Making sure your logo reflects your brand

Broadly, there are three ways you can get a logo designed: you can do it yourself, use an Internet template or hire a designer.

Doing it yourself means it will only cost you your time, you control exactly how the logo will look, but if you are not a graphic designer, even with the best intentions it may well end up looking like a dog's dinner (which may be fine if you are launching a pet food brand!). An Internet template or logo maker service will deliver a logo based on how you respond to their prompts about colors, shapes and fonts. These are very affordable (from $25-$245)[77] but they don't allow you to add any strategic direction in the development process so you may end up with a very professional looking logo that lacks a real connection to your brand. The final way is to hire a designer to develop your logo. This allows you to shape its development, to work with a trained professional and be assured that the results will be unique to your brand. For a rough guide, to work with a freelance designer to create a logo and provide the files would be in a range of $245-$735 a day and the task would take three days. Design agencies are the next step up and are very useful if you have a larger organization with multiple design needs.

However, it's a false economy to try and create a logo cheaply because, as well as appearing on all your materials, its role is to be an asset for your brand, almost like a visual ambassador communicating your story. It's also very often the starting point for a larger design process – my own projects always begin with the logo before moving onto the website and marketing materials, for example, and so these will naturally reflect the logo, good or bad. So it's important to invest in getting it right. Bear in mind the cost of developing a logo with a designer will still only represent a fraction of the other costs you will have to consider, like manufacturing your product, building a website, creating packaging, producing marketing materials, hiring staff, leasing premises, etc.

I happen to love working with designers. I have not yet met one who isn't extremely talented, creative, thoughtful and considered. They are not, however, brand strategists but very often that's the role they are asked to play, as they have to second guess what the brand stands for and what the brand wants to communicate.

This, of course, is not a good use of a design resource as much time can be wasted developing designs based on what the designer, in the absence of clear direction, thinks is the best approach. For the client, there's no way of knowing objectively which designs can support the brand because the brand strategy has not been expressed. This often leads to new rounds of design being required, and so in effect, the design process itself becomes a way of developing the brand strategy. This can take up a lot of time, and time is quite often how the designer is paid, so it will be more expensive for you as the customer. Furthermore, you are placing the development of your brand into the hands of a person whose expertise is in design and not in brand strategy. Bigger design agencies can have brand strategists, but these often come with a bigger price tag.

Designers absolutely love to be given clear direction and I'm hoping that this book will mean a lot more designers are given a lot more direction. It will mean time spent designing and not time spent developing a brand strategy. Coming to a designer or a design agency having taken the time to write your own brand strategy will mean you can give clear direction, you'll know the elements of the brand reflect your truths as you have written them, and you'll be able to judge objectively if the design recommendations will work because you'll have the brand strategy to use as a benchmark. (I always tell clients when working with a designer on a new logo that all the recommendations will be right – all will be "on brief" – and so it becomes an exercise in building consensus around a single option.)

Providing direction to a designer can be done very simply by providing the following three-part design brief that shouldn't take up more than two pages.

- The first part defines the design task, what is it that you need – a logo, a website, a brochure, product packaging, an app. By being very specific about what you need the designer will be able to give you an accurate idea of the time, and therefore the fee, to deliver it.

- The second part introduces the core elements of the brand strategy – the brand vision, positioning, brand proposition and values as well as an introduction to the type of sector you are in – its themes and challenges. You can add to this the tone of voice of the design you would like and any other considerations there may be – like your biggest competitor uses red packaging so avoid that color.

- The third covers who you want to target and what you want them to do. So, you'll describe the type of person or company you want the brand to engage with and what sort of response you want the design to elicit.

We look more closely at defining audiences in the next chapter.

The role of color

Blue is THE color, I absolutely love blue! I once heard that Giorgio Armani said wearing navy blue is very slimming[78] – this made me love blue even more. My firm recommendation is that the best logos are always blue. However, you may not agree. You may prefer red, and your co-founder, green. Colors are subjective. Yes, there is a great body of academic and scientific work that tells us what each one represents and how each color may make us feel, but at the end of the day, we cannot help but be drawn to certain colors. It's part of how we are made. So, how do you develop the color of the logo objectively? My advice is to ask your designer to develop the initial routes (I think a choice of three is plenty) in black, white and gray, which will mean you are looking at the design and not being distracted by colors. Once you have landed on a route or two then color can be introduced.

Here's a whistle-stop tour of the world of color:

Red is the color of blood and fire. It's intense and can be seen as the color of passion, danger, power and energy. It's very stimulating and is often used on websites for the 'click to buy' buttons, for example. Blue, on the other hand, is thought of as calming, stable and ordered, and is usually used for large corporates and banks. Green is, of course, linked with nature, but it can also symbolize growth, harmony and safety, and is often used by brands in the healthcare sector. Yellow, the color of the sun, is associated with joy, happiness and energy. Purple is affiliated with royalty, ambition and luxury. Orange is seen as a creative color, one that represents enthusiasm and encouragement. Black, as well as being associated with power and death, is also very elegant and probably the color of your designer's turtleneck. Finally, if black is dark, then white is light, innocence, purity – some say, the color of perfection.[79]

I would, however, use your designer as a guide. Have a look at your brand values and use an established color reference to explore how you might assign colors to your values (red for confidence, blue for stability, for example). Review your sector, see if there are any dominant colors and use those if you want to be seen to belong or don't use them if you want to stand out. Bear in mind that you want the logo to be distinctive and too many colors may make your logo appear muddled – looking at the Interbrand 100 best global brands, over 80 percent of the logos featured use only one or two colors.[80] Worth also looking ahead to think of what your needs are beyond the logo; you can use color to represent your different products or services, and as a way of signaling different aspects of your brand or different sections on your website – often called a color palette – so perhaps you may want two colors for your logo and a further three or four to provide you with some versatility in your brand presentation. These don't have to be different colors, but possibly different shades, textures or halftones.

A brief word about shapes. Just like colors, there is a meaning behind them that works on a subconscious level. Squares and rectangles are the shapes we

> *"Every facet of your logo needs to be able to tell a story about your brand that is authentic, directional and true."*

see most of in our lives and so represent familiarity and safety, circles don't have a start or an end so can suggest eternity or energy, and the triangle can deliver direction and movement. Again, look at your brand strategy and see what shape or combination helps amplify the elements of your brand.

To summarize, every facet of your logo needs to be able to tell a story about your brand that is authentic, directional and true to the brand strategy. If the brand is about integration, the elements should engage with one another. If it's about delivering clarity, there should be clean lines and sharp edges. If the brand is about pushing boundaries, then look to the creative and energizing colors. If it's about providing security, consider colors that communicate stability and consistency. That's not to say a customer will always recognize that in the logo, but it is about you or your team knowing that the logo has been created to express the brand strategy, that there is nothing superfluous about its presentation, however clever, cool or beautiful your logo ends up being!

Case study: Weaving the brand into the fabric of retail

Blue Yonder is a software company based in Karlsruhe, Germany that specializes in delivering pricing and replenishment solutions to the retail sector, driven by their own proprietary artificial intelligence software.

Their solutions take a myriad of data sources (from the weather, the time of year, promotional activity, etc.) and predict with an extraordinary degree of accuracy what the demand will be for every single product in a supermarket – that's around 45,000 products in a typical supermarket!

However, up to late 2015, the brand served a number of sectors and so the job of the brand strategy was twofold:

- To help Blue Yonder better engage with retailers, who tend to only want to deal with other retailers and are suspicious of anybody from outside their industry – let alone a bunch of data scientists!

- To ensure that the internal culture was able to embrace this shift and really get behind this single-minded focus.

Of course, focusing on retail made sense – just think of how your own shopping habits have changed in the last two years, let alone the last ten! It's a sector that is scrambling to keep up with customer expectations fuelled by a heady mix of digital innovation and brands like Amazon and Alibaba that are seemingly re-writing the rules of retail on a daily basis. So anything that can help retail meet customer expectations and deliver on the bottom line is worth looking at.

Together with their senior management and marketing team, we used the brand strategy process to do four things differently.

Firstly, we stopped focusing on the science and started focusing on the problems the science could solve. Don't say how it's done, say what it will do! It's a common challenge, particularly with tech companies who will often focus on how the solution is delivered and not what the solution delivers. And yes, it is compelling to share how the solution is delivered as it's often the thing that differentiates one tech brand from another. So it has its place but not until after the benefits of the solution are communicated. Retailers are generally not that interested in the science but they are very interested in how they can reduce operating costs, increase margins, create value, all of which will be relevant and provide the motivation for them to ask, well how can you do this?

Secondly, we gave up re-inventing the wheel by creating standardized messaging templates that ensured teams could get on with selling and not having to keep inventing ways of talking about the brand. Usually, the first question on an RFP (Request for Proposal – the process that a sales team will need to go through to be considered for a project) is to define what the company does. Not always easy, but if there is already a standardized message in place it makes it a lot quicker to do. In fact, a great deal of RFPs ask the same questions, and so by having a resource where those questions have already been answered means consistently more accurate proposals that allow the team to focus on what will win the business.

Thirdly, we re-developed the brand to reflect the retail world – for it to feel like it is part of the fabric of retail through its choice of language, imagery and identity. We did an exercise in the workshops where we explored what color would best represent the corporate world – the answer being blue. We then explored what color best represented the world of retail – with the answer being anything and everything! This helped us see the need to move the brand identity that was predominately blue to one that could be seen to engage with all kinds of colors, and so reflect the retail sector it was serving.

Fourthly, we changed the language of the brand. Retailers like to talk to retailers and use a language specific to their sector. This is not unique as it simply reflects that fact that, in effect, if you speak my language you will probably be aware of my problem and will be in a better position to help than someone who doesn't 'speak retail'. This doesn't mean a website full of jargon, but it does mean referring to their challenges in their language and labeling your solutions so that they are understood by the customer. And by language think words, images, infographics. The images showed customers not just shopping, but enjoying the benefits of the store, so a shopping bag full of fresh ingredients, on the shoulder of a customer on their way to cook dinner.

The resulting brand strategy and evolved brand identity were introduced to the teams across the network, a new website was launched along with a suite of new communications products, sales teams were equipped with the new messaging, even the office interiors were re-designed to ensure their focus was always top of mind.

BRAND ARROW QUESTIONS

These two questions both relate to your logo and can be answered once you have completed your Brand Arrow.

BA15: Pick a logo that you like and are familiar with. What do you think are the three things the logo wants to tell you?

Take your favorite brand. Spend some time looking at its logo and work out what you think the brand is trying to tell you. Is it easy or hard to see the connection between the colors and shapes in the logo and the reason for its success? Now review its website and marketing communications. Does the logo feel like an integrated part of the brand or just stuck on? Now do the same exercise with the brand leader in your sector and the brand that you feel is your closest competitor.

BA16: Take your current logo. How much of the brand strategy is it telling you?

Look at what the key colors in your sector are. Is there a dominant color? If there is, what is it and why do you think that is? Where does your logo fit in that sector? Does it tell customers the brand is firmly in the sector or does it say you are removed from the sector and have a different point of view? Review your brand strategy, list out the positioning and values. First, assign what colors and shapes match them and then look to see if any are represented in your logo. If you had to make a presentation, and all you had was a chart with your logo on it, could you tell your brand story? This exercise will tell you if your logo lives up to your brand strategy. If it doesn't, there is a strong case for you to use the brand strategy to provide direction for a designer to create a new or evolved logo for your brand.

CUSTOMER

CUSTOMER

The key audiences and the characteristics they share

POSITIONING

PROPOSITION

VALUES

PROBLEM

SOLUTION

BENEFITS

FEATURES

DISTINCTION

VISION

9. AUDIENCE
Who the Brand Will Engage With

THE KEY MESSAGES IN THIS CHAPTER:

- Your team is your number one audience.

- Brands have to engage the culture of the organization.

- The brand needs to really understand its customers.

Back in the 14th century, John Lydgate had become a monk at the Benedictine monastery of Bury St Edmunds at the age of sixteen. He was a prodigious writer, and over the course of his life penned a number of books, translated many works from Latin and wrote a great deal of poetry.[81] Some 600 years later a few of his lines still remain in our popular culture – you may have found yourself quoting John Lydgate whilst describing your attempts to convince a thrifty friend to buy a round of drinks as "getting blood out of stone".[82] It is said he also wrote, "You can't please all of the people all of the time,"[83] to which I would say why would you want to anyway? I always hear alarm bells when I'm told by a client they want to sell to everybody. Everybody does not exist! It's just not possible to have a brand that everybody wants, so why spend the time and money trying to reach them when you only need to really engage with a much more modest number of people.

Of course, every organization will have an audience to engage with, regardless of type, location or ambition, and defining that audience – often referred to as the target audience – is a critical part of developing and marketing a brand. It stands to reason that the better you know the type of individual or organization the brand needs to engage with, the greater the chance of creating features and messaging that will appeal to that audience. Just as importantly, by defining the target audience you also have a much greater chance of being able to find them!

> *"Everybody does not exist! It's just not possible to have a brand that everybody wants."*

If you have a brand that is aimed at businesses, it is most likely that you will target companies that you feel will benefit from your brand. Within those companies, there will be departments that will be applicable to what your brand delivers. So an accounting software program will be of interest to the finance department and a new printing company will most likely want to connect to the marketing department, for example. Within those departments there will be various roles, some of which will be relevant to you, and others not. And there will also be roles within the company that have the authority to make decisions about potentially purchasing your brand – sometimes these roles might be within the department but this is not always the case. By building a database of companies that might be willing to buy your brand and by understanding who the user and purchaser will be, you can develop a strategy for reaching them. This will likely involve developing a description of their job roles and needs, often called personas, which will help you to identify the media channels that they use and the sort of content that will be relevant to their needs. We look at this in more detail in chapter 12 on the sales process.

In this chapter we are going to focus on the different ways you can define audiences that are not businesses but are customers who are using your brand for their own private use – shoppers buying the weekly groceries, those wanting a latte in a high street coffee shop or searching the Internet for the best deal on car insurance, for example. But before we do that we will look at your most important audience – your team.

It starts with your team

The team responsible for creating and representing your brand to customers has to be the most important audience because your customers will engage with the brand through the products your team creates, through the content they produce and the experience customers have in dealing with them. It's a big risk to commit the time and resources to creating a brand if your team, especially those in sales and marketing, is not engaged in the development of the brand or are only exposed to the strategic rationale for it. And for this to happen, attention needs to be paid to how to engage the team in the brand strategy process and how to engage the team in its delivery. For these things to happen, we need to acknowledge the close relationship between company culture and brand strategy.

Organizational culture can be described as unwritten rules or an unseen force that shapes patterns of individual and group behaviors, which are consistently repeated. Richard Perrin, a partner and Head of Advisory at KPMG Romania, defines organizational culture as "the sum of values and rituals which serve as 'glue' to integrate the members of the organization."[84] And the sum of these shared values, beliefs and assumptions are reflected by how people are expected to behave and interact, how decisions are taken, and how work activities are done. Edgar Schein, a professor in organizational behavior has identified three levels of culture, all of which have the potential to impact and be impacted by brand strategy.[85]

The first he calls "artifacts" and these describe the physical and behavioral attributes that are easy to see – the workplace environment, what people wear and how the staff interact with one another. So an office where everybody wears suits and calls each other by their surname will have a different culture to one where jeans and T-shirts are the default uniform and everybody uses their first names. One is not better than the other but they are clearly different. The second he calls "espoused values" and this refers to how the culture is legislated through an organization's stated values, vision and its processes. I remember wandering around The Body Shop factory many years ago where every available wall had a quote from its founder Anita Roddick. By the end of my visit, I had a very good idea about what drove and informed the culture of The Body Shop. Schein's final level is called "basic underlying assumptions" and these are the unseen and not consciously identified interactions that shape the normal everyday behavior between team members – they are so far woven into the fabric of the "way we do things" they are invisible, even to those in the organization![86]

So, a brand strategy will have an influence and be influenced by the culture of the organization. We want it to celebrate and encourage the

> *"To have real impact, a brand strategy needs to be created, accepted and accessed by those charged with delivering it."*

positive elements of an organization's culture and attempt to address any negative cultural issues. This can only be done if the process of developing a brand strategy is collaborative, encourages engagement and ensures that participation is acknowledged. For the team to be asked their opinion, to be listened to and then see how that opinion is represented is a powerful "by-product" of the process. This is a very good thing because, as already stated, to have real impact, a brand strategy needs to be created, accepted and accessed by those charged with delivering it.

Getting to know your audience

Understanding who is going to want to buy your brand and then using that understanding to shape your sales and marketing is essential as it ensures you are using your resources as effectively and efficiently as possible. It will stop a brand trying to convince a middle-aged man that he really needs a pack of ultra absorbent nappies or that a keen classical music lover would like a pair of tickets for a heavy metal festival! There are a number of ways to understand an audience, and we'll summarize three commonly used classifications, all of which are pretty accessible.

The first and most common is demographics, taken from the Greek words *demos* meaning "the people" and *grapho* alluding to a description[87] – it's a way of categorizing an audience into various segments. Age is a very useful way of defining your audience, and it can be done by life stages – adolescent, teenage, young adult, adult, middle age and seniors – or by generations – baby boomers, generation X, millennials. This will give you an idea about what sort of things they will be interested in and whether your brand will be relevant to them. Gender is useful too, as men and women do differ in some of their buying habits, from the obvious differences in, say, clothing preferences, to more nuanced differences like attitudes to charity giving, for example. Income and

Occupation is another that looks at the buying power of customers, and as with all generalizations there will be exceptions, but you need to be sure that your target audience can afford to buy your brand! You can find demographic data in most countries by accessing census websites, which are usually free of charge.

The second is geographic. Location can be a clear steer for a brand. Many businesses rely entirely on their location to be successful and build their businesses around serving a community - hairdressers, estate agents, accountants, restaurants, funeral directors, etc. all meet a local need. To find out if your brand will succeed in a specific geographical region, take some time to visit the area and count the number of businesses that already provide the sort of service your product or brand is offering. This classification can also include the actual geographic features of a location - you won't find many surf shops in London but there are plenty on the coast of Cornwall. A particular region may have a high percentage of a demographic that your brand might appeal to. Because of the large number of technology and social media firms in Silicon Valley, it is likely to have a larger proportion of younger, relatively affluent adults than, say, Florida. It's not to say that there are not any young affluent adults in Florida, it's just there is a great concentration in Silicon Valley which means they are, in theory, easier to reach. Different regional cultural preferences also have a part to play. I remember a trip through Maine where we stopped for lobster at the roadside McDonald's, and you can buy a beer with your Big Mac in France or have your burger served in a pitta bread in Greece, for example.[88]

The third type of segmentation is attitudinal, which tries to find out how an audience sees the world. These attitudes can be captured by doing market research to explore the motivations and opinions on a whole range of subjects and products. It's actually relatively easy and inexpensive to submit questions to a weekly national survey that captures the views of an audience, very often segmented into different types - just google research omnibus. This quantitative method (large numbers of people answering questions online or on the phone, often with a yes or a no) will give a broad understanding of an audience's attitudes to things that could impact their willingness to buy a particular brand. For a more accurate idea you could commission qualitative research, where a researcher will often engage with a small number of precisely targeted customers to get a deeper sense of their views. This approach, whilst being more accurate, is significantly more expensive and time-consuming.

Leveraging the influencers

During my MBA year back in 2000, I was part of an incubator that generated ideas and business plans for new dot-com start-ups. We came up with an idea of an app called "Like It Want It" that allowed you to buy any item you came across during your day that took your fancy. It could be a bottle of wine at a restaurant, the watch a friend was wearing, a jacket worn by a fellow team member; all you had to do was take a photo of the item and the app would purchase it for the best price it could and deliver it to your door. In effect, it was trying to make the idea of a shop redundant! The idea was sound, if a little ambitious, its just the technology wasn't there, smartphones weren't fully with us, and the word app was yet to be invented! Of course, the idea of the power of recommendation is as old as the hills. Take my friend Tim, for example. We go running, sometimes work on projects together and have similar interests. He is my guinea pig, and by that I mean a lot of the stuff that he buys first I end up buying second because I trust him and he knows me and knows what I like. I have taken my family on "his" holidays, hired suppliers and even bought cars based on his recommendation. And I'm not alone; we all have a number of friends like Tim whose opinion we value.

Technology has now enabled the Tims of this world to influence not just their friends but millions of people who they have never met by sharing their recommendations on social media. These influencers are not usually aligned to any one brand; they are trusted by their audiences, seen as independent and credible, and so are very powerful. And whilst the big brands are very keen to get their products recommended by these social influencers, the principle works for smaller brands too. My nephew Tom is the co-founder of a very cool brand of sunglasses called Finlay and Co. The brand is growing fast but because all their profits go back into designing and manufacturing, their budget for marketing is slim. So the team sends out sets of complimentary sunnies to a small and select group of celebrities in the hope that some will wear them. And importantly, be seen to be wearing them. Tom tells me that when an actress by the name of Meghan Markle was featured on the front cover of a national newspaper sporting a pair of Finlay's sales doubled in a day! But the beauty of the story is that whenever Meghan, now the Duchess of Sussex, is photographed for the media wearing sunglasses – whatever the brand – their sales go up!

The idea of endorsement is part of how we all make decisions, whether it's rating a purchase from an Internet provider to ranking a restaurant – in fact, you may have been persuaded to buy this book by the endorsements on the back cover or from the feedback online or even the recommendation of a friend. So, when defining your audience, it's worth exploring who might your audience be influenced by and how you might be able to secure their support.

Case study: It's all about the T-shirt

Do you remember the story of Blue Yonder from the last chapter? Their artificial intelligence software delivers extremely accurate price and replenishment predictions to the retail trade. The brand strategy guided a new presentation of the brand that was "fit for retail".

However, there was a problem. The data scientists, who made up the majority of the workforce, didn't like it!

They had been fully supportive of the process and understood the rationale to focus on retail, they agreed the new brand strategy would help the firm be successful in that sector, but they didn't have an emotional engagement with the new brand. It left them cold.

Their networks and culture were not the same as the "go to market team"; one focused on the external market, the other on the world of data science, and in their eyes, the brand didn't engage with that world. In fact, one data scientist told me he wouldn't wear a Blue Yonder T-shirt at a symposium because he didn't feel a connection to the brand when around his contemporaries.

And I got it!

Did that mean we had got it wrong? Had the brand strategy failed in in engaging with all the internal team? No, but we did need to find a mechanism to make the brand chime with all the different cultures at Blue Yonder, not just the "go to market team". So we ran workshops with a mix of disciplines to get a sense of what was working for them and what was not. The key insight that came from those workshops was the discovery of the tension between the inquisitive, experimental mind of a data scientist and the company mandate to approach problems in a structured way that delivered business efficiencies.

Put another way, the data scientists kind of liked re-inventing the wheel!

The spirit of exploration was part of the DNA of discovery and this needed to be defined and expressed. It did not mean changing the brand strategy, but rather acknowledging and celebrating the attitude of all members of the team that built and sold their solutions.

And that's exactly what we did. We took the spirit of exploration and used the brand strategy to create a name for the team at Blue Yonder. We called them "Beyonders" – always exploring new possibilities, looking beyond the current horizon. The name was presented in a similar style to the new identity and shared with the teams in the channels that worked best for them – stickers and T-shirts!

This kept the integrity and focus of the retail brand but allowed for an emotional engagement by recognizing the culture of those charged with delivering its solutions. It didn't change the need to deliver business efficiencies but did acknowledge a different perspective. And it looked cool on a T-shirt too!

BRAND ARROW QUESTIONS

BA17: Categorize your top three target audiences.

List your top three target audiences based on their importance to your brand – you can rank them in terms of the revenue they bring to the brand or the market share they represent, for example. Under each, write a paragraph that provides a sense of who they are. You can use demographic data like age, gender and income; attitudinal information that captures their views on key market and societal subjects, and if it's a business customer you can define their role in the organization. What matters is that by the end of this you have a clear sense of the type of customers you are wanting to engage with.

BA18: What five characteristics do all your customers share?

We have talked about the role of the brand strategy as sitting above the component parts of an organization (different customers, products, markets, etc.) so that it can corral those differences into a cohesive whole. We now need to take the work done in segmenting the audiences and capture the common themes or threads that run through them all. I find an effective way of doing this is to write each audience type on a flip chart, put them next to each other, stand back, look to see the commonalities that characterize all your audiences, and make a note of the top five.

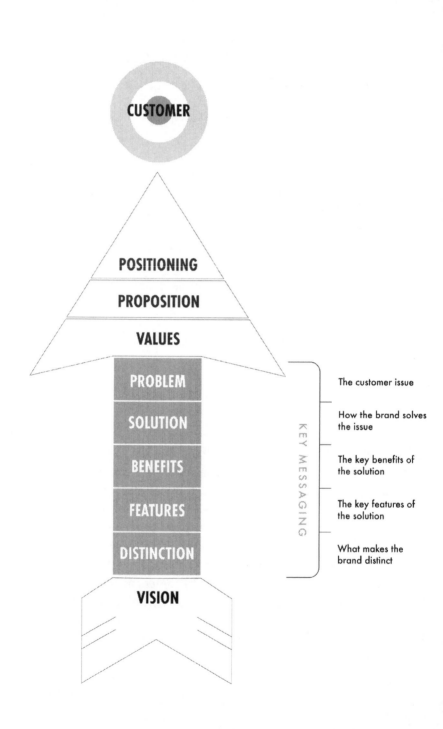

CUSTOMER

POSITIONING

PROPOSITION

VALUES

PROBLEM — The customer issue

SOLUTION — How the brand solves the issue

BENEFITS — The key benefits of the solution

FEATURES — The key features of the solution

DISTINCTION — What makes the brand distinct

KEY MESSAGING

VISION

10. MESSAGING
What the Brand Will Say to Its Audience

THE KEY MESSAGES IN THIS CHAPTER:

- To be relevant, you need to solve a customer's problem.

- You need to solve it in a way that makes you stand out.

- Always lead with the why before the how.

Like many of us, I'm keen to support locally grown produce. So imagine my surprise and delight at finding the store up the road had managed to do just that. I know this because they had put up a sign saying locally grown citrus fruit. However, on closer inspection, their clementines had, in fact, made a 6,000-mile journey from Peru to make an appearance in the store. Duty called, an assistant was found, and whilst he claimed never to have heard of Peru, did agree it was highly likely that the continent of South America was in fact not around the corner, but a very long way away. The sort of opposite of local really. Smiles all round, the sign was changed, the assistant had discovered the existence of Peru and vigilance had saved the day.

Getting the message right is of course very important, and especially challenging for those with inherently complex messages. In this chapter, we will look at how you can use the brand strategy to define and then structure your messaging so that the point of your brand is crystal clear.

Be relevant but be different too

"Just what is your problem" might sound like the start of an argument but it's a very healthy way to begin to think about creating messaging, because you are asking yourself what is the problem that you can solve for your customer. This may seem like an easy question, but it really isn't, because your customers may have lots of needs – or their needs may differ from

> *"By defining the problem, you are on your way to creating a brand that has the capacity to be relevant to all your customers."*

one to the next. However, for the brand strategy to work, we need to identify an overarching need that all your customers face.

By defining the problem, you are on your way to creating a brand that has the capacity to be relevant to all your customers because, once you know the problem, you can deliver the solution. And that makes you relevant. Without knowing what the problem is, your brand is just a list of features and benefits that a customer has to wade through to work out why you might be relevant to their needs. You won't find many willing to do this.

So, once you have captured the problem, you then need to describe how you are going to solve the problem. The Brand Arrow question in chapter 5 asked you to do just that, so it's worth reminding yourself what you wrote. Once you have done this, the task of deciding how to structure your messaging – in effect, what you say first and what you say second – is made easier because you are now responding to the problem you have said can be solved.

However, it's not enough just to be relevant, you also have to be sufficiently different from other brands also wanting a customer's attention. What makes your brand better qualified to meet their needs, what makes it more relevant than your competitors? If every brand was as relevant as the next, then how would a customer be able to discern why they should choose you? So, when expressing how you are going to solve the customer's problem, you need to include the element that makes you different or distinct from everybody else. Here's an example taken from a brand strategy delivered recently for a client providing software solutions to the legal industry.

A significant problem facing many law firms is that their expertise is by and large wrapped up in individuals who would likely command a high salary, need to be billed out at a high rate, and by definition are limited by being just one individual. The answer is a relatively new field where the expert imparts their knowledge into a software program that can then be accessed 24/7 either by the law firm themselves or by their clients, saving both time and financial resources. We expressed their need and the solution something like this:

> Need: The demand for legal expertise has never been higher and whilst automation software can deliver convenient access to expertise it can be expensive, time-consuming and complex to deliver.

> Solution: Our expertise automation software does not need programmers to build it, so it is easier, faster and less expensive to build and so maximizes the reach and profitability of your expertise.

Once we defined why this particular brand was both relevant to customers and different from the competition, we were able to develop a message hierarchy that started with the benefits of the system and then went on to define its features.

The role of a message hierarchy

Let's open the dictionary to remind ourselves that the words "benefits" and "features", whilst being closely linked, are very different. A benefit is "something that is advantageous or good; an advantage", features, on the other hand, are "prominent or conspicuous parts or characteristics". The customer experiences the benefit of your brand when they use it to solve their problem. The brand's features are the way the problem is solved, they are not in themselves the benefit.

This may seem like semantics but it's very important to distinguish between the two because quite often we get them the wrong way round, focusing first on the "how we do things" and not the "why a customer should be interested". In a message hierarchy, the benefits come before the features, just like the horse comes before the cart. However, most companies feel at ease talking to a customer about how they do things and not why they do things. They will talk about the process to get to a solution or the different features of the product before they talk about what benefits that process or feature will deliver. The cart before the horse.

"The brand's features are the way the problem is solved, they are not in themselves the benefit."

Focusing first on the how, and not the why, makes it very hard to sell to a customer. Why? Because there is no reason for the customer to listen to you as you have yet to give them a reason to. Until you give them that reason to listen, you are not relevant and so will find it hard to get and keep their attention. By first of all defining the benefit, you have a captive audience because self-interest is at play here – you are seen as relevant because you are solving the customer's problem. This gives you permission to then describe the features of your solution – you can describe the cart!

By placing the benefits first, you are in effect saying to the customer, the brand knows what your problem is and can solve it, are you interested? Once the brand is seen as relevant we can then answer the important question of how we deliver those benefits, how we solve the problem – the features.

When putting together a message hierarchy for a client I always start by reminding myself what the customer's problem is and how the brand plans to solve their problem. I then look at the internal drivers, the things the client is already really good at doing, and then add to that the benefits they deliver to the customer – making sure I include tangible evidence that the solution does actually work. Now I have a long list of benefits and my aim is to end up with five in total so that may mean incorporating similar benefits into one point or even dropping the more peripheral ones.

To start to get to the hierarchy, I work out with the client, of those five benefits, what two we could live without. These will be numbers four and five on the list. We now have the top three and need to put them into an order, and for that it's simply a question of asking what is the first thing you would mention to a customer? If we were to write a sales deck what would be on the first chart? Or, if we were to rewrite the website homepage, what would be the headline? What would follow the headline? It doesn't really matter how it's done as long as we end up with a list of five benefits that starts with the most important and ends with the least important.

Once the benefits are defined and ordered I then turn to the features and do a similar exercise, aiming to have a hierarchy with the most impressive or influential feature first and so on down to the fifth. In some cases, each benefit has its own set of features, in which case I have a slightly different approach where underneath each benefit there is an ordered list of the features that deliver that benefit.

Once done, you will be well on your way to creating a message hierarchy that will direct the copy you write for your website, sales decks, social media messaging, etc. The two Brand Arrow questions at the end of this chapter will ask you to define and prioritize your features and benefits, and the Brand Arrow questions in the final chapter will guide you in the development of your message hierarchy.

Building a brand boilerplate

The antidote to re-inventing the wheel is to make sure everybody already has the wheel, and they know what it's for and how to use it.

Companies can waste a lot of time and resource re-doing messaging for different tasks (like the website or a sales presentation), possibly because they don't know that the messaging has already been done, or they don't think it's right. Going through the Brand Arrow process means that the messaging that has been developed is based on sound strategy and is focused on delivering a clear point to the customer. The way I recommend my clients do this is by creating a brand boilerplate. This is a Word document whose role is to ensure the whole organization can understand what the brand strategy is all about and then to apply that understanding both internally and externally. If it is written well and care is taken in engaging all parts of the organization it will increase turnaround speed, deliver a consistent brand story and encourage self-sufficiency.

The brand boilerplate is tremendously useful as a tool to engage the whole organization in the brand strategy and provides a whole host of benefits to reduce colleagues' workload. And once you have completed your Brand Arrow pretty much all the content you'll need will either be done or will take not much time to be created.

Typically, the first section will introduce the rationale for the brand strategy and its component parts. It will then go on to focus on the customer, detailing their challenges and how the brand can help them meet those challenges. The following section will contain the key messaging for the brand and will be supported by customer quotes, proof points and brief customer case studies. The final section will go through each product or solution along the lines of what are the benefits, what are the features and what do they deliver. Throughout the brand boilerplate there will be sections of different lengths and detail that can be cut and pasted into other documents.

Say your sales team is writing an RFP (Request For Proposal), a common requirement from most prospective customers, which takes up quite some time to complete. A lot of questions are the same from one RFP to the next – company background, product descriptions, proof points, etc. – and all of this information can be housed in the brand boilerplate; the sales team simply needs to cut and paste from the relevant sections.

Or your PR agency wants to describe how one of your solutions works in a press release, provide a potted history of the firm and some quotes from happy customers. With the brand boilerplate the agency can write 80 percent of the release before having to take up your valuable time – and of course the quicker releases can be written the lower the fees!

It's also very useful as part of the on-boarding process for new starters. Whether it's something to be read that defines the brand or it forms the basis of a presentation, it will go a long way to helping that new starter get a sense of the organization they are joining.

I have found this approach makes the development of sales and marketing materials so much easier and quicker because the strategic focus, the messaging priorities, product descriptions, proof points, etc. have all been worked through and defined. Yes, of course, each activity will need to be tailored to each audience, but you can be assured that the brand will be represented accurately and consistently. This approach also means you are not in the business of re-inventing wheels!

Case study: The Trojan Horse

Do you remember the film, *Monty Python and the Holy Grail*?[89] At one point on their quest, the intrepid knights, having unsuccessfully laid siege to a castle, had the cunning idea to build a giant wooden rabbit and leave it outside the gates for their enemy to then wheel in. The idea, taken from the famous story of the Battle of Troy,[90] was that by hiding in its body until night, they could leap out and attack the fort from within. The joke was of course that the knights forgot to actually get into the rabbit and so their plan failed.

The real story of the Trojan Horse is a good illustration of how you can use a messaging hierarchy to compensate for a perceived weakness in an organization, to "hide" a flaw by focusing on a strength. You do this by emphasizing the strongest or most relevant aspect of the brand at the expense of the perceived weaker part of the brand story.

I used this strategy with a client who provides data storage to some of the world's biggest brands.

Data centers have been around since the 1950s[91] – remember those images of huge rooms full of whirring machines with blinking lights and spinning tape spindles? Those images are usually seen now with a caption stating that all that computing power can be found in the smartphone in your pocket.

As computers shrank in size, their numbers and power increased, and when the Internet took hold there was a need to provide the right environment to maintain the servers they ran on – safe, cool and with an uninterrupted power supply. This led to the advent of the data center – vast chilled halls full to the brim with servers. Some companies built their own but most, due to the huge cost involved in building and maintaining them, located them in external data centers, sometimes called co-location centers or carrier hotels.

This particular client was a pioneer of the sector and over the decades had built new data centers around the world to meet the seemingly never-ending demand for off-site computer power. For many years it was the leading light in the provision of secure off-site data storage.

But as time went on, and with the phenomenal increase in demand for data, innovations like cloud storage and advances in technology, new entrants came into the market and took over the mantle of leadership both in terms of innovation and market share.

Although it had strong brand name recognition and a good global network, it had slipped from being known as an innovator to one best characterized as "solid but sleepy". However, with the near completion of its newest data center built on its London campus came a brand opportunity. By dint of this data center being the newest in the world it was also the most innovative and with that came the chance to start to reposition the brand as an innovator by imbuing the values of this new data center across the whole brand.

So how did we go about this "imbuing"? With a message hierarchy.

Firstly, the original naming of the new data center was very individual and clearly communicated innovation. It was clever, but as it did not include the name of the brand it belonged to it did not help our cause. It was changed to include a reference to the main brand so that every time the data center was written about, so too was the brand. Innovation by association.

Secondly, we ensured that every marketing campaign either started or finished with messaging around the innovations of the new data center, regardless of the topic in hand. For example, we created a campaign that focused on global thought leadership, and we referenced the innovative data center as an example of how the brand was looking to the future and leading by example. Every positive attribute was presented in the context of innovation.

Thirdly, we offered "hard hat" tours of the data center as it was being built – allowing prospective customers the chance to meet with the architects and designers of the worlds' most advanced data center. In actual fact, the innovation was experienced not through the fabric of the building site but through virtual reality tours that demonstrated the benefits of its innovations in a way that in itself was innovative. These hard hat and virtual reality tours were strongly promoted across all the sales and marketing materials. In fact, the virtual tours became a firm favorite with the sales team at events and presentations.

So, not quite a Trojan Horse, but a way of framing the brand story through a single lens of innovation. This led the business to start to shift the mantel of "solid but sleepy", to become more innovative in how it delivered its services, and be able to compete more effectively with the newer global brands. It also delivered a 97 percent rise in leads to the sales team!

BRAND ARROW QUESTIONS

BA19: Prioritize your five most important benefits.

To start with, go to the work you did for Brand Arrow question 6 in chapter 3 on your internal drivers, the things you are already really good at doing, and jot down those ones that relate to what you deliver to your customers. Now look at your services and add to the list the benefits they deliver to the customer – make sure you include tangible evidence that what you deliver does actually work! You'll end up with a list – try and keep that list to no more than five items. Now prioritize the list as directed in the chapter.

BA20: Describe the features that enable the benefits to be delivered.

Think through or discuss with your team the features that enable each benefit to be delivered. Perhaps first of all note all the features and then put them into an order of the effectiveness – ideally you want to aim for around three per benefit. If you find you have one benefit that has five or six features it may be worth considering whether the single benefit could be split into two.

11. MARKETING
Getting the Brand Into the Right Hands

THE KEY MESSAGES IN THIS CHAPTER:

- A marketing plan is a roadmap for the brand to head toward its destination.

- Marketing delivers the brand to your customers.

- A plan will define the budget and keep you accountable.

Every time the player stepped onto the basketball court he was fined $5,000. This would unsettle any player, let alone one that had just made the transition from college to professional basketball. However, the player was Michael Jordan and his trainers were made by Nike.[92]

Nike had already started to sponsor players, at the time (back in 1984) a radical move as most sports brands sponsored teams, not individuals. But by finding players who embodied their values, Nike was able to associate its brand with the rising success and fame of a pool of young and precociously talented athletes. Over time, these athletes became de facto ambassadors for the brand and still include the likes of golfer Tiger Woods, tennis player Roger Federer and footballer Christiano Ronaldo.[93]

Nike, however, had taken the idea of sponsorship a step further by creating a brand of basketball shoe called Air Jordan, named after the seemingly impossible time Michael Jordan would spend in the air and not with his feet on the ground. But why the fine? Well, the shoes were red and black after the colors of his team, the Chicago Bulls, and not the regulation 51 percent white as required by the NBA at the time. Nike paid the fine, along with an initial sponsorship deal worth $7m.[94] It was money well spent. Despite Michael Jordan's retirement as a player back in 2003, the Air Jordan brand is far from retired, pulling in $2.86bn in revenue in 2018.[95]

This story is a testament to the fact that Nike has a strong sense of what its brand stands for (I would say it's based around a single-minded pursuit of sporting excellence) and it uses marketing to great effect to amplify that brand message to the audiences that most identify with it. So marketing, to paraphrase the American Marketing Association, "creates, communicates and delivers a brand to its customers" and Nike has been doing a very good job of this since it changed its name from Blue Ribbon Sports in 1971.[96]

Mapping out a plan

Before focusing on brand strategy I served as a marketing director in both the US and Europe, and it really is a fantastic role, but like every senior job in business, it has its fair share of challenges and curve balls. For me, keeping the sales team topped up with qualified leads was a constant worry, as was getting a glimpse of the product road map so that we had enough time to prepare the marketing for new launches. (It seems only people in marketing actually know how long it takes to create campaigns – it is always a genuine surprise to non-marketers when told, for example, it will take three months not three weeks to create a marketing launch for their new baby.)

Stopping agencies from spending vast sums on new campaigns when the first one was still only a year old was a familiar battle, as was the seemingly constant flow of marketing materials developed by the other departments instead of using what was already developed for that express purpose by the marketing team! Finally, I don't miss the annual fight for budget with the financial director, who tended to really, really dislike marketing because we spent lots of money on things that were either hard to understand or hard to quantify. I found the best way of dealing with these challenges was simply to develop a marketing plan, either on my own or in partnership with the team, to get that plan endorsed by the boss (or my line manager depending on the size of the organization) and then to share it with all the different people the plan would impact.

A marketing plan is a roadmap for the brand to be able to head toward its destination. It will deliver a framework to help you prioritize your activities

and ensure you are con-
tributing to the aims of the
business. It will give you a
good sense of what fac-
tors inside and outside the
organization you'll need to
contend with, and help

"The role of marketing is to respond to the requirements of the organization, so it's essential to define what those requirements are."

you keep on track by defining a set of measurable goals and objectives. Critically it will mean you can construct a budget and justify why you need it, it will tell you what sort of content you will have to create and the best channels for getting that content to your audiences. If there is just one of you and the budget is tight, all the more reason to make sure you spend those precious resources the right way, and if you are in a larger organization, it will be the means by which you can share what you are planning with your colleagues.

There are many kinds of marketing plan, and many good books written on the subject, so in this chapter I'm going to share a five-step process that reflects the principles I have used in my own role as marketing director. The good news is that you already have a lot of the content you will need to create the plan through the process of answering the Brand Arrow questions.

1. Business – what you do and how you do it

Firstly, you need to put the plan into context because the role of marketing is to respond to the requirements of the organization, and so it's essential in a marketing plan to define what those requirements are. Every brand will be part of a market or sector. This might be an emerging market, or one that has been around a long time, or it could be part of the service sector or manufacturing or the charity sector. Whatever sector the brand is in, there will be forces shaping it. Take some time to consider how the market has changed over the last 10 years (or a shorter period for an emerging sector), its growth or decline, the number of customers it serves and the sort of products or services it offers. Now consider how the sector might look in another 10 years, and try to identify what would be driving these changes. There are many different techniques for doing this, and the one

I would recommend is "PESTLE", with each letter representing a different factor that will have an influence on the sector - political, economic, social, technological, legal and environmental.

I also find it useful in this section to describe, with one or two sentences for each, how your products or services are developed, how they are brought to market, and what is the process of developing new products or services to keep pace with evolving sector. Finally, grab a copy of the business plan, or if one does not exist or is off limits, sit down with the boss or your line manager for 30 minutes and find out what the organization wants to achieve. Because your marketing plan will be using up your organization's resources, by yoking the plan to its ambitions you are at least attempting to ensure they are being invested in the right place. I always summarize this section by defining the key themes in the sector and the key needs the brand will need to meet.

2. Environment – the internal and external factors to consider

Next, you'll need to define what the challenges are within the organization and in the sector it is operating in, looking at the factors that are within your control and the ones that are not. A good way of doing this goes by the acronym SWOT which stands for strengths, weaknesses, opportunities and threats. This has been around for donkey's years, and there are many different approaches, but for our purposes this works well and can be applied both internally and externally. We have already looked at our drivers and barriers (chapter 3 on brand vision) and it would be useful to have these in mind as you go through this exercise. Of course, you don't need to use this structure (or for that matter any structure) but I'm a big fan of structure as I think it gives you the freedom to be creative and innovative because you have a strong and thorough foundation to build on.

So, make a list of the strengths inside your organization. This could be the quality of your product, the experience of your team, etc. Externally, the strengths might be the fact there is a rising demand for your services and the stellar reputation of your brand, for example. Do the same exercise for weaknesses. What are the challenges internally that will need to be overcome, and externally, are there characteristics of the sector that undermine your chances for success? Opportunities could encompass things like a competitor's poor quality, a change in government policy, and internally, the funding for a new line of products has just been approved.

> *"The marketing plan has to amplify the brand strategy and connect the brand to its customers."*

Threats might include a sector-wide reduction in pricing, a new competitor launch, changing consumer habits or a key member is leaving the team, for example. Aim for about five bullet points on each and then look to put them into an order of priority. This exercise, along with the work done in step 1, will shape how you develop your goals and objectives because they are a response to the internal and external environment you are in.

This section should also take a close look at the other brands in your sector. By auditing your competitors you will gain great insights into what brand and marketing activity works and what doesn't. You will be able to identify the gaps in the provision of services and gain a good sense of what is already being done and what could be done better.

3. Brand strategy – expressing the point of the brand

The marketing plan has to amplify the brand strategy and connect the brand to its customers and so I always include a summary of it in the marketing plan. I suggest you keep it to a minimum and just focus on the four elements that make up the core of a brand strategy. You will want to briefly define the role of each element and then state what each represents for the brand in question. Given we have spent a good portion of this book defining what a brand strategy is, I thought it would be more instructive to give an example of how you can summarize one in a marketing plan.

The example is taken from a recent assignment for an organization that uses local radio in an innovative way to reach remote farming communities in Africa. The need the brand is meeting is that very often, smallholder farmers do not have the information they need to improve their farming skills or sell their produce for a good price, which means they remain in poverty and are vulnerable to any crisis. Farmer's Voice Radio trains local organizations to disseminate up-to-date, relevant and practical information to these remote communities. It does this by bringing local farmers, agricultural experts and supply chain partners together to share their knowledge, experience and expertise on the radio. So here's the summary:

Brand vision – what we want to achieve: To transform the lives of millions of smallholder farmers through a highly effective and cost-efficient strategy to engage farmers in the production of local radio programs that broadcast vital farming information, so improving the long-term viability and sustainability of rural communities.

Brand positioning – the two words to sum up the essence of what we do: Seeding knowledge. (By using local radio we enable farming communities to access and share the knowledge they need to succeed.)

Brand proposition – how we express that to our stakeholders: Connecting farmers with knowledge.

Brand values – our character and work ethic:

Empathetic – taking the time to fully understand farmer challenges;

Practical – knowledge gleaned from the field to be put back into the field;

Local – local solutions to local problems;

Accessible – from the home, in the local language, in a medium that is free to use and to re-use;

Adaptable – to the changing challenges of rural farming communities;

Sustainable – embedded in existing local institutions.

This example shows how a brand strategy anchors the marketing plan and provides a lens for the team to see how marketing can deliver the brand into the right hands.

4. Stakeholders – who the marketing needs to be aimed at

This section provides a summary of your stakeholders, broken down into your primary and secondary target audiences, as well as detailing those you want to influence. We spent a chapter looking at this subject and so, again, I think it's more instructive to provide an example of how you can summarize your stakeholders, so let's continue looking at Farmer's Voice Radio.

> Primary audience: Program managers at organizations largely based in developing countries, operating as closely as possible to smallholder farmers, for instance, local non-government organizations implementing agricultural programs, farmer membership organizations/cooperatives, radio stations serving rural communities and government agricultural departments.

> Secondary audience: International organizations with operations or supply chains involving smallholder farmers in developing countries, often via some of the same local intermediaries mentioned above. These could be international non-government organizations, agri-businesses, research institutions, certification schemes, networks, etc. Or donors interested in the same.

You will see that the primary audience focuses on the "on the ground" local intermediaries who will engage with rural communities, and the secondary audience focuses on organizations that are a level above, whose remit involves encouraging improvement in the sustainability of rural farming. This division is helpful because it tells the brand the kind of materials, subject matter and language to adopt for these two separate audiences.

5. Goals, objectives and a budget – defining and measuring what to aim for

What you can say with certainty is that marketing does need money! There's the sunk costs of producing materials – websites, brochures, events, social media campaigns and sometimes advertising, and there are the fees involved in paying suppliers to build, write, photograph, film, record, post and monitor it all. It's an investment that if done well will deliver many benefits to the organization, and if done badly will hinder the organization in meeting its goals. So, setting targets and measuring the progress in meeting those targets is good financial stewardship.

This can be done by defining a set of goals (what you want to achieve) and objectives (how you will achieve them). Having a time span of between 12 and 24 months is the most practical time period for planning purposes. Limiting the number of goals to three is the most manageable and will allow you the best chance of delivering them, and for each goal I usually assign no more than five objectives. Each objective should include a means by which you can measure your progress (called Key Performance Indicators and Key Development Indicators – we looked at this in chapter 4). By defining goals and objectives you will have a clear idea about the tasks you have to deliver (lead generation, brand awareness, content creation, new product launch, store openings, for example) and the channels you have to be able to deliver them (social media, advertising, product endorsement, point of sale materials, for example).

When sharing the plan with the wider organization, acknowledge the business ambition and then summarize the brand strategy as this provides a strategic response to that ambition. Then define the goals and finally list out how the objectives will deliver each goal. For your team, do the same but for each objective spend time developing how you will be able to execute each objective; agree the KPIs and KDIs. Once you have done this process, you have a 12-month delivery plan.

All this will mean you will be able to plan ahead and ensure you have the right team in place, or access to the right suppliers, to deliver on those goals. Very importantly, this process will enable you to put together a budget to deliver on those goals, and provide you with a strategic rationale for your budget which you can use to justify your request to the big wigs, or your bank, or your co-founder, for example.

So you now have in place everything you need to execute the plan. You know the dynamics of the sector and the goals of the business, you have analyzed the internal and external factors that are shaping the organization, you have summarized the brand strategy, understood your key audiences and put together a set of goals and objectives that cover the next 12 to 24 months, and detailed what type of activity marketing will be engaged in to contribute to the ambition of the organization. This process has also delivered an idea of the budget you will need.

One final point is to make sure you share the progress marketing is making across all departments – something that in my experience is not widely done. Often I find that employees don't really know what marketing is up to, but they do know it takes a lot of budget. So, taking a lesson from the corridors of my daughter's primary school, I always encourage clients to display forthcoming campaigns and their results in the common areas so the whole company can see what the marketing team is focused on.

However, quite often I'm told this is already being done on the intranet or through emails, which is fine but I find putting up cork boards with the latest press releases, or a preview of a new campaign, is incredibly effective at sharing what the marketing department is doing with the company's hard-earned cash. Staff kitchens are a great place to communicate with the organization – something to read waiting for the coffee to brew, for example, and there's usually more than one person in the kitchen so it can spark conversation and debate. Which is what marketing is all about.

Case study: Lorna's legacy

Despite the fact that Lorna as a teenager had been diagnosed with a life threatening heart condition, here she was, in her mid 40s, full of beans and passionate about the box of fair trade coffee she had just placed on the table.

It was 1991, filter coffee was still sold in boxes and fair trade was something that nobody in the UK had ever heard of. Lorna Young was here to change all that.

Fast forward 25 years or so and fair trade is now big business, worth $4bn in sales worldwide, with over 1.4 million farmers across 74 countries engaged in creating over 30,000 products all of which are certified fair trade.[97]

Lorna worked for one of four organizations that had come together to create the UK's first fair trade coffee company, with the great name Cafédirect. Her goal was to get the brand into every supermarket chain in the country – a task that she managed within a year of launch as it happened. My job was far simpler, to create and deliver the marketing to launch the brand with the princely sum of £4,000 (that's less than 0.02 percent of the total marketing spend in the industry.[98]

However, we had a good story, one that nobody had heard before, we had the clout of the supporters from the four organizations, we had a genuinely delicious product, and of course we had Lorna.

At the time I was working for a fabulous agency whose clients were exclusively good causes. My job was to persuade some of London's most creative advertising and design talent to work with these clients for nothing in exchange for a warm glow and a chance to stretch their creative muscles. Oh yes, I also had to ensure what small budget I had for marketing was multiplied at least one hundredfold.

The really big challenge, however, was around the messaging. Even back then, charity fatigue (where people are just tired of being asked to donate to yet another charity campaign) had set in, and on top of that, charity products were not known for their quality. Does anybody remember Campaign Coffee? Bought once, drunk once and then left in the back of the cupboard to wait for the end of time, or to be thrown out when the kitchen was renovated – whichever was sooner.

With Cafédirect we did, in fact, have a great product and a great story. Simply put, by buying Cafédirect you were paying a fair price to the people who grew the beans, and in return you got a great tasting cup of coffee. We were fortunate to find a young creative team (who later become very big cheeses in the ad world) to work with us and they understood the fine balance that was needed. Of the launch ads, the one I remember that best captured the spirit of the campaign was of a positive image of a grower with the headline, "Bring rich smooth coffee into your home, and a little sunshine into hers". This light touch communicated a quality signal – the promise of good coffee and a promise that the coffee would do some good too. The copy went into a little more detail and the messaging of the campaign set the tone for defining the new fair trade movement that was not charitable but had the interests of the grower at heart, and the interests of customers too.

We targeted what we coined as the semi-ethical consumer – not the typical charity shop customer but a well-to-do (the coffee was a premium priced product), intelligent and brand savvy customer who knew that the brand values embodied would reflect positively on them.

It worked. Lorna's hard work with the supermarket buyers, the campaigning from the four organizations, along with the light touch messaging and some very generous media owners delivered a 3 percent share of the filter coffee market in the first year.[99]

Since then, Cafédirect has grown into a company with sales in excess of £12m, it has won countless awards for its great coffee and social model, it has a range of filter, instant and pod coffee, and it even sells tea! As well as helping to usher into the UK the fair trade movement it is still pioneering the way we work with farming communities – it donates 50 percent of its profits back to producers, that's on top of the fair trade premium, and producers sit on its main board.[100]

The Cafédirect brand was and still is an extremely valuable asset for the organization. At launch, it used marketing to make the complex issue of fair trade understandable and relevant for customers. It also recognized that people like to do good and be seen to do good too, and so targeted an audience that valued what the brand said about them. The brand also provided a way of coalescing its four owners and thousands of supporters in support of a single and compelling call to action – to be stocked in all the supermarket chains. Since then it has built a commanding market share and reinforced its ethical credentials. It's a brand that is visible in the supermarkets and trusted by its customers.

Lorna, who passed away in 1996, I'm sure would have been pleased but I'm also sure she would ask, what next?!

BRAND ARROW QUESTIONS

BA21: Define your competitors' brand strategies.

By auditing your competitors you will learn a great deal about them which will help enormously as you develop your own brand strategy. Start by making a list of the market leaders, those that have been in the sector the longest, the new entrants, brands that are not doing so well, and if not already captured, your direct competitors. You'll want to end up with a list of up to a dozen brands to review. This exercise will provide some great insights into what brand and marketing activity works and what doesn't, if there are any gaps in the provision of services that you could fill, and give you a good sense of what is already being done and what could be done better.

For each brand, open their website and you will most likely land on the homepage. In theory at least, this should contain the most important elements of the brand. It's a bit old fashioned to think of the homepage as a shop window but its role is to marshal the most valuable assets of the brand into a single place that will tell the customer why the brand is both relevant to them and different from others. Before scrolling down or clicking any of the links, look to see if there are any words under the logo, and what is the main headline and visual. If there is copy make a note of it along with how they structure their navigation (this is a great clue for where they see their priorities). Now draft what you think might be the brand proposition for each one.

BA22: Rank your competitor's marketing by quality and relevance to your brand.

Next, put yourself in the mindset of a prospective customer and spend time auditing each of your competitor's websites. Visit each page, be sure to review their most recent press releases and downloadable content and if you are feeling cheeky, subscribe to their newsletter. Capture their range of services, what kind of evidence they provide to substantiate their claims, and define the type of customer they are targeting. Note down their primary and secondary messaging and how the benefits and features of its product range are defined. I like to review all the brands in one go, usually on a large board divided into columns or a series of flip charts, as this will help you compare one to the other and provide a useful overview of the sector. Score out of 10 how well each one does in terms of brand and marketing activity, then score each one in terms of relevance to your own brand. This will provide you with a very useful way of seeing the type of brand and marketing that works in your sector, what to consider emulating and what to avoid.

12. SALES
Everybody Needs to Sell

THE KEY MESSAGES IN THIS CHAPTER:

- Sales is a process not a vocation.

- The better you know your customer, the better chance of a sale.

- Don't waste your time selling to those who don't want to buy.

The elevator pitch, so the story goes, came about because that was the only time you got a chance to see the boss, when he or she was riding the elevator to and from the management suite, so you had better get your story straight and deliver it during that short trip.[101] The good news is that these days there are more opportunities to get your message across to the CEO – many offices are now open plan, most CEOs will actively seek out staff views and there's the "always on" social media channels. The bad news is that along with the opportunities social media affords us, there are a great many more distractions – our attention span is dropping through the floor; in 2000 it averaged 12 seconds, now it's 8![102] So, the need to pitch an idea quickly, to get to the point and engage the audience is still a very useful skill, in fact, it's still very much in demand. I know this because I was asked to pitch the idea of this book to publishers. Admittedly, it was a 100-word email and not an elevator ride, but the principle is the same. This is what I wrote:

Points are good because they stick into things.

Every brand needs a point, a sharp definition of its purpose that will stick in people's minds.

This means making a choice about what that one point is. Brand owners find this fiendishly hard to do.

A brand strategy can do this. This book introduces the Brand Arrow, an easy to follow process to enable every reader to write their own brand strategy.

Each Brand Arrow contains the brand vision, tagline, values, key messages and customer profiles that will ensure the brand will hit its target and make the right point.

> *"Everybody needs to sell, whether it's an ice cream product, a professional service or an idea for a book."*

So you see, everybody needs to sell, whether it's an ice cream product, a professional service or an idea for a book. And selling can be tough. It requires insight and discipline to marshal your resources to present the best possible offer you can, and determination to keep going when the push-backs happen. It's hard for sales professionals, and it's doubly hard for those who are not – and I count myself in that category and my guess is that most of the readers of this book will too. So how can non-sales people be really good at selling? Most importantly, by demonstrating you believe in what you are selling. It's an overused word in business, but you really do need to exercise passion for your product or solution. But of course, passion won't win the day unless it's yoked to a process that you trust and follow.

So in this chapter, we are going to break down the sales process into a series of six manageable chunks to give you an idea of the steps needed to create a sales plan and provide the best chance of making a success of sales. You may well be doing some of these steps already, others may not be relevant, or you may have a team responsible for sales. No matter, it's useful to look at the strategy behind it, the role marketing plays and how brand strategy can contribute to sales. It's based on my experience of running my own business and having to find and pitch for new client work. It also draws on previous marketing roles where I supported both consumer and businesses' sales. Finally (and most importantly), the process contains the wisdom of friends and colleagues who have worked very hard at becoming successful salespeople.

Before we dive in, a word about terminology. So far we have not distinguished between creating a brand that targets businesses (known as Business to Business, or B2B) and a brand that targets consumers (Business to Consumer, or B2C) because there is no difference in the brand strategy development process. With sales, however, we will see that some steps require a specific B2B or B2C approach and where that is the case, they will be flagged.

Whilst we're at it, one more clarification. So far in the book, I have used the term customer to refer to the external audience the brand needs to connect with, but in this chapter, we will need to distinguish between customer and consumer. Most B2B brands use the word customer to refer to the person or organization being sold to, and we will do the same, and it also makes sense to refer to the target of B2C sales as the consumer. The only wrinkle here is when a B2C brand sells to a business like a wholesaler or a supermarket, for example, it will use the term customer. So, to be crystal clear, a B2C brand can sell to a customer (to stock its brand) and a consumer (to buy the brand). A B2B brand just sells to customers.

Final, final point: Just like the brand strategy process, the sales process is iterative, so conclusions drawn for the first step will always need to be reviewed in the light of knowledge gleaned in subsequent steps.

1. Offer – what it delivers and what it costs

We have already captured the need you are addressing and how you plan on meeting that need. In so doing we have expressed the problem in a way that makes it sufficiently different or distinctive from other brands in the same sector. Part of the sales process is to put together what is called "the offer" which will define your key benefits and features both in terms of the impact they will make and the value they will deliver. The session on key messaging in the appendix will help you develop your offer.

Once you have defined the offer it will need to be validated to make sure your audience will think it's worth paying for, and if it is, how much would they pay? This will involve doing research into the market to understand what the current price range is to have this problem solved. You will then need to find out how much appetite there is to pay for your new/different/ better solution, and the best way to do this is to talk to potential users of your brand about your solution and explore how much they may be willing to pay. Or you can commission research which can be done inexpensively and quickly by using a national online omnibus survey where you can purchase a number of questions to an audience who you believe would be interested in your brand.

Once you get a sense of what people are prepared to pay you'll need to understand if that is going to deliver enough income for you. For that you will need to know how much it will cost to deliver your solution. For example, the cost of manufacturing, the value of your time, the investment needed to market the solution, etc. Bear in mind price can be an effective promotional tool. For example, if you want to quickly grow your customer base to generate economies of scale or demonstrate there is demand for your product, you could offer it at a low price or even free of charge. This will deliver volume but not much value. Alternately, you could price your solution to generate greater value, your customer base will grow more slowly but it will deliver greater margins. Once you have defined your offer and its price you can move in to explore the size of your potential market.

2. Market – defining how big your opportunity is

This stage is about getting a realistic idea about the number of people who might consider buying your product or service. You'll start big and work your way down to a number that is realistic – this is referred to as your addressable market. Let's say you are selling a brand of organic wine, and the total number of people who would be eligible to buy your product is 20 million. But of course not everyone likes wine, in fact, you know (from research) that only half the population drink wine so you are down to 10 million. You also know that wine drinkers are evenly split between those that only drink red and those that only drink white. Your wine is red so it will appeal to 5 million of the population. One last thing, because your wine is organic it is much more costly to produce so you are planning on charging a premium, and you know that only 20 percent of wine drinkers are willing to pay a premium. The exercise tells you there are 1 million people potentially interested in your product – this is your addressable market.

This is useful to know for a number of reasons. Firstly, it stops you selling to people who don't like your product – in this case, there's no point in trying to sell red wine to someone who only likes white wine. Secondly, it can tell you what the total value of your addressable market is. For example, those 1 million premium red wine drinkers buy a bottle every month, for an average price of $20, so your market is worth $240m. Thirdly, it allows you to set a sales target that will either be based on what you need to sell to make a profit or what you need to sell to become an established brand in the market. Finally, and related to the last point, the process will help you determine a price point for your offer.

3. Route – identifying how to reach your market

Now that you know you are targeting 1 million wine drinkers you can look at how you reach them. B2C sales can either be direct or indirect. In our example, the wine brand could sell direct to consumers by having a stall at local farmers markets or perhaps selling on an Internet platform like Amazon Marketplace. By selling directly you are maximizing your margins, but what you save you may well end up spending promoting your brand to consumers. It also takes time to build up awareness of your brand amongst your target consumers. Most brands go down the indirect sales route and sell to an intermediary, like a supermarket or a bar, who will buy your wine and then sell it in their stores or serve it in their bars. These will be your customers. You get to your addressable market faster but the value from your sales is smaller because, of course, these intermediaries take a hefty margin (so having a clear idea about how much income you need to generate from intermediary sales is essential). For both approaches, however, you will need to spend time and resource building awareness of your brand to the consumers who will drink the wine, and in the case of intermediaries, the customers who will be stocking your brand.

B2B sales offer a different set of options. You can sell to a trade retailer who will buy at a discount and sell to their own customers, a reseller who would be the face of your brand to their own customers or a co-seller who will sell your brand along with a host of their own added-value services. Sticking with our fictitious organic red wine brand, a trade retailer could be a cash and carry that would stock your brand for its own trade customers (supermarkets and bars, for example). A reseller would market your brand on your behalf (they may have a license or an exclusive agreement, in a geographical region you are not able to operate in, for example). A co-seller might service the restaurant trade by providing wine selection consulting, tastings, the wine itself and storage equipment.

4. Personas and profiles – knowing who you are selling to

In B2B sales, personas identify the roles or type of profiles that you need to engage to win a sale. Each of the senior roles in a business will have a different persona, a different set of responsibilities that your brand will need to demonstrate it can meet. So the persona is a mix of the job description – the tasks they are charged with delivering – and their needs – the stress and strains you can help them overcome by buying your services. A persona plays a vital role in the sales process because you will need your brand to engage with different customers with different roles. There are many different personas in a business, but for this exercise, it's useful to focus on the two personas that any sales process will need to address. The first is the business buyer. This persona has the problem the brand will solve and so the messaging could be around the benefits of the solution. The second is the economic buyer, the role who will fund the purchase, or make a business case for the funds to purchase it, so the messaging here would be more about the cost, time for implementation, etc. The actual job title of these two personas will depend on what services the brand is delivering.

For B2C, we are primarily interested in building up a picture of the person we are targeting so that content can be created that will be relevant to their needs and interests. There are a myriad different ways of defining a B2C audience, for example, by their life stage – are they working, retired, raising children, etc. – by their income – how much disposable income do they have and what do they spend it on – by their interests – are they sporty, do they go to festivals, love to travel, etc. The better you know your consumer, the more likely you will be able to engage them. (It may be worth a quick flick back to chapter 9 on audience where we looked at this in more detail.)

5. Outreach – creating and communicating the right content

For B2B sales there are a great deal of options to start to engage with your prospective customer. For example, you could commission a report based on a relevant industry topic, or write an article that tackles an industry issue in a fresh way (sometimes called a White Paper). You might produce a series of short articles and paragraphs that could be promoted on social media platforms like LinkedIn, Twitter, Facebook or your own site – usually referred to as social selling. You could offer a chance to watch a key team member's presentation via the web (known as a webinar), or you could go old school and invite prospective customers to a workshop with an industry expert. Finally, taking a stand at a trade show is a great way of meeting your customers face-to-face and seeing what the market and your competition is up to.

> *"Quite simply, without a lead, there cannot be a sale."*

Whatever you do, the key is to create content that your prospective customer is going to see as valuable, and by understanding the personas you want to engage with, you will have a much greater chance of doing so. And if that content is seen as relevant and valuable, your prospective customer will want to download that report or come along to a workshop. To do that, they will be willing to provide you with their contact details, and once you have their contact details you have a lead, and leads are the foundation for every sales plan ever written and implemented! Quite simply, without a lead, there cannot be a sale.

In effect, there is a value exchange going on here: you want the contact details of your prospective customers so that you can start the process of selling them something, they want the content you have developed because they see it as useful in being able to do their job. What that means is the content cannot just be a sales pitch for your brand, it needs to deliver something that is thought leading, objective and relevant. In my experience, you can communicate your key messages but it needs to be done with a lightness of touch, if it's heavy-handed it's not likely to deliver an engagement.

The value exchange for B2C is actually not that much different. Instead of using content as a way to generate leads, here the content is used as a mechanism to create communities of interest, groups that share an interest either in your brand or an interest related to your brand. By creating content that demonstrates your brand is relevant to them, consumers will be more likely to engage in your content and ultimately buy your brand.

Whether your outreach program is aimed at a B2B or a B2C audience, it also needs to grow awareness of your brand. If the brand is known, consumers are more likely to trust your brand and buy it, and the business customer more willing to come to you with a problem that you can solve. For brand building, you can be much more focused on your key selling messages because it requires their attention not their willingness to share their details with you. So your brand building may include Google ad words, advertising on relevant sites, a campaign of tweets and posts, for example. Again, by understanding who you are targeting you are much more likely to know their media habits and so make an impression on them.

6. Conversion – turning a lead into a sale

Once you have a lead, you need to understand whether it's useful or not; remember you are making it as easy as possible to generate leads and so, some will have the potential to become customers but many will not. You don't want to waste your time or resource on a lead that will never become a customer, so you need to qualify the lead. There are all kinds of systems to do this but basically it comes down to the following:

- Does the lead belong to a company that could become a customer? It may not be in the right sector, it might be too small or big, it might be in a different country, for example.

- Is the lead senior enough to make a financial decision or recommendation? If not, then there is no point in pursuing it.

- Does the lead actually have the problem that your brand is addressing? If they don't have a need then they won't buy the solution.

- Is the timing right? It may be the budget has just been used up, or the business has just bought from a competitor, or the company has been taken over.

To be able to qualify a lead, you will need to do some research into their company, get a sense of why they downloaded the content they did, and in all likelihood, you will need to speak to them. As a rule of thumb, the harder you qualify a lead, the smaller number of leads get through, but those leads are much more likely to merit the investment of time and resources needed to convert them to a sale.

Quite often up to this point, the sales team have not been that engaged in the process, it's usually the role of the marketing team to generate qualified leads because the process of outreach is a marketing function. Once the lead is qualified it is handed over to the sales team whose job it is, ultimately, to win the customer's business. This process is often referred to as the sales funnel.

The outreach program used to generate leads will still be a very useful source of content for the sales team as they begin to build relationships with the qualified lead – with the goal of identifying if there is an opportunity for a sale in the next 12 to 18 months. If there is not, the sales team will most often place the qualified lead into what is called a nurture program, where the company, through the marketing team, will stay in touch using the outreach program until such a point as the situation is right for them to be handed back to the sales team as a qualified lead.

If there is a realistic chance to make a sale, then the sales team, working with their own specialists (the product team for example) and the relevant prospective customer teams, will develop a proposal, or respond to an RFP (Request For Proposal) that will include the timings, costs, the specific solution and its implementation. The customer will use this to decide whom they should appoint (this process is pretty much always competitive). This is called the opportunity and it is the final phase of the sales funnel, and because of the investment made by the sales team and the customer, the conversion rate to a sale is much higher than in any other stage – sometimes as high as one in three.

So, here the whistle-stop tour ends. Clearly, the subject of sales is a big one, and there are many, many books written about it, usually by very successful salespeople (I know this because the books I have read always start by stating how successful the author is!). By definition, a single chapter in a book about brand strategy can only skim the surface, and so if you need a more in-depth guide to selling, I suggest you read Mike Weinberg's excellent book *New Sales. Simplified: The Essential Handbook for Prospecting and New Business Development* – it does exactly what it says on the tin.

Case study: Lady Luck at the movies

He was the sales director for a company based on the East Coast of the US. I was the newbie, flown in from the UK to spend lots of "hard-earned by sales" money on marketing, or so it seemed. I had developed a brand and marketing strategy for the management team and after some discussion, I was asked whether I would come over and implement the recommendations. This was, of course, terrifying. As a consultant you tend not to do too much implementation – it's all about listening, stringing together some ideas into a report, handing it over and moving on to the next client. Actually doing something tangible was a big step up!

However, a few months later we sat facing each other discussing the thorny question of how much budget should be assigned to marketing and how would we know if it was being used effectively. After much discussion, a plan was hatched that would mean every time the sales team converted a lead that was generated and qualified by marketing, the marketing budget would receive one-third of the value of the contract for one year. The company had an excellent sales team, a clear idea about the size of its market and a good sense of their customer personas. What they didn't have was a coherent brand that would support their sales and marketing efforts.

We set to work developing a brand strategy and used it to guide the development of a new logo, packaging, marketing materials and, once that was done, our first outreach program – a series of advertisements that played in movie houses across the east coast. During the first week of the campaign, sitting in the audience, was the main buyer for a large chain of supermarkets who called the next day to enquire about becoming a customer. The sales team did a great job in converting that interest into a large order, and in fact, to this day, that supermarket chain is still their biggest customer. So, along with a large slice of luck, I got my marketing budget and the sales director went on to become the boss!

BRAND ARROW QUESTIONS

BA23: Using the answers from previous Brand Arrow questions, put together a messaging hierarchy.

On the top of a flip chart, copy out the answers you gave to Brand Arrow questions 9 and 10 from chapter 5 (what is your customer's greatest need and how do you meet it?). Label the first sentence PROBLEM and the second sentence SOLUTION.

In slightly smaller text, note down the answers from Brand Arrow questions 19 and 20 from chapter 10 (prioritize your five most important benefits and describe the features that enable the benefits to be delivered). Label those two lists BENEFITS and FEATURES.

Now write out five sentences that start with a benefit and end with a solution. When you are done, go to chapters 4 and 11 and review what makes you different from your competitors (Brand Arrow questions 7 and 8, 21 and 22). Make sure your message hierarchy feels distinctly yours.

Finally, stand back, and with your right arm give your left-hand shoulder a pat – congratulations, you have just completed your message hierarchy!

BA24: Write a brand proposition based on the message hierarchy.

The end goal is to have a sentence that sums up the best, most compelling and relevant expression of your brand, what we referred to in chapter 5 as the brand proposition. With fresh flip chart paper, write down your brand positioning (Brand Arrow question 7 in chapter 4). Use the recently completed messaging hierarchy and your brand values (Brand Arrow questions 11 and 12) and take the first key message and see whether this could be used as a brand proposition – is it the right length (around six words), does it represent all the brand or just one feature, does it reflect the brand values.

Work through each key message and you will find either one of those lines works, or as is more likely, it will be a combination that will deliver the brand proposition. It's best to do this with a team as you can bounce ideas off one another. You'll see this task has been left to last so that all the exploration of the brand strategy has been completed.

CONCLUSION

Well, we made it! You have read this far, and I have written this far. Well done to us both! So here's a roundup of what we covered.

We first of all made a distinction between brand and brand strategy. We defined brand as a product or a service that delivers a consistent and distinctive benefit to a customer, containing a set of characteristics to differentiate itself from competitors and ensure it remains relevant to its customers. We characterized a brand strategy simply as a framework for you to make good choices. Its role is to discover, define and order the key elements of your brand story before you start to communicate them; to define the single most important thing about your organization, its character and its values.

We then looked at the four elements that make up a brand strategy, the first being the brand vision, whose role is to state the destination of your organization. This is critical because if the brand strategy is going to support and equip you to head toward your destination, there must be clarity about where that is. The vision itself should be big, broad and long. Big because it's about the journey toward the vision, not the arrival. Broad, because it should cover the impact of your collective efforts and not be the result of a single one. Long (term) to avoid getting stuck in transactional details by focusing at least 10 years ahead. We also covered the idea of carrying out an audit of your capabilities to get a good sense of your drivers (what you have that will help you get to your vision) and your barriers (what you will need to change or stop doing).

The brand positioning defines the essence of the brand, expressing in one or two words what makes the brand uniquely yours. For me, it's the most important part of a brand because it's the root from which everything else grows. Like a rudder that is unseen but directs the ship, a brand positioning is written solely for the team charged with creating and delivering the brand, and it helps to make sure you all know the course the brand is taking. And by reducing the number of words used, you end up with a potent and concentrated source from which to draw from. The brand proposition follows this and is around half a dozen carefully chosen words that will capture the positioning of the brand in a way that is clear, honest and motivating. It is written for all who have to understand and use the brand. Think of it as the start point for the story of the brand, in effect, a guide for the team to present the brand consistently across different audiences. It provides an introduction to the benefits that all the brand's products or services deliver.

The final element of the brand strategy is the brand values, which describe the character of your organization. How it behaves, how it treats its staff, the tone it uses in communications, how it presents itself to the world, and the products or services that it produces. Externally, they should be influential, shaping how the brand is developed and how it is experienced by customers. Brand values help customers recognize your brand, reinforce the relationship they have with it, and critically act as a benchmark for the brand to live up to. Internally, brand values play a vital role in keeping you focused on what your brand stands for, helping to deliver a cohesive experience for customers, differentiating the brand from others in the sector, and sometimes acting as an antidote to problems you are trying to solve.

We then spent some time exploring how the brand strategy can shape the tools you have at your disposal to create and deliver the brand.

We acknowledged that a good name is an open door to your organization but a bad one means that the door is closed.

That every element of your logo should tell your brand story, it's the start point of all your marketing communications.

We saw that the most important audience for your brand is your team and to be successful it needs to engage the culture of the organization.

That the messaging needs to be both relevant to your customers (to meet a need) and different from its competition (or else why would they choose you). And to always, always lead with the "why" before the "how".

That the marketing plan is a roadmap for the brand to head toward its destination, that it will deliver the brand to your customers, define the budget and keep you accountable.

And finally, that sales is a process, not a vocation, and that the better you know your customer, the better chance of a sale. But don't waste your time selling to those who don't want to buy.

So we are done, and I do hope this has been illuminating for you. It is my sincere wish that this book will guide you in the development of your own brand strategy and that you will reap the rewards of being able to clearly define your point to all those who need to help you grow your brand and those who will use it. The appendix will take you through how you draw on your responses to the Brand Arrow questions to complete your own Brand Arrow.

And to finish where we started. Points are good because they stick into things, and every brand needs a point, a sharp definition of its purpose that will stick in people's minds. And that's the point of this book.

WORKSHOP CHART

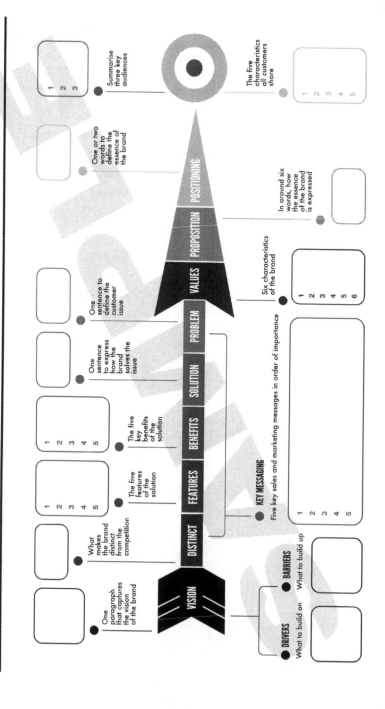

APPENDIX 1
Building Your Brand Arrow

You have answered the Brand Arrow questions and have your responses to hand. Great! Or maybe you have considered the questions as you read through the book and have a sense of how you would answer them. Also great! The purpose of the questions was to create a pool of knowledge that you can draw from to equip you to complete the Brand Arrow and so write your own brand strategy. You can do this by filling in the 14 text boxes contained in the Brand Arrow Workshop Chart. Head to my website, **brucemmckinnon.com**, provide the ISBN number (found on the page with all the publishing information at the start of the book) and you can download a chart as a print-ready file.

The tools you'll need

A pen

Preferably a marker pen, and some flip charts too so you can stick your thoughts on a wall, stand back and ponder what you have written. I find that speaking out thoughts that are swirling around the brain is a great way of moving that thought into something useful. Writing them down is the next step because you have to choose the words you are writing down and that is, of course, the purpose of all this, to help you make good choices about how your brand is defined.

Time

When I run a Brand Arrow workshop I allow a solid eight hours to complete it, so we end the day with a brand strategy. You don't have to do that but I do suggest you carve out time without distractions – maybe a series of two-hour sessions on a weekday morning, or take one question at a time. Having to complete the Brand Arrow to a deadline is useful as it will focus the mind and ensure you make the choices you need to instead of putting them off for another day.

Brevity

I love business author Stephen Covey's approach to focus. He writes: "The main thing is to keep the main thing, the main thing". All through the book I have asked for one sentence, a list of five things, one word, etc., with the intent that in the process of distilling down to the bare minimum you only keep the stuff that is important. This requirement continues in completing the Brand Arrow, and to help you in this, I'm suggesting that all your submissions should fit onto a Post-it note. (The rectangular ones are best as they give a smidge more room than the square ones.)

Company

If you have a team, then they will love you for listening to them and asking them to participate. I always find that the collaborative process of developing a strategy is as powerful as the results themselves.

If it's just you, that works too, but be ready to be really honest with yourself, don't try to do it all at once, and every now and then, go find a friend and share your progress – verbalizing your own rationales to someone else really helps clarify your thinking.

Patience

Don't worry if the answers don't come immediately – you are investing your time in a process that is proven to work. I know because, as well as developing it, I have used the process dozens of times with clients and yes, I still get stuck on occasions and always say to myself, "Trust in the process, Bruce". So, if you hit a brick wall, write out the best answers you can come up with, and then go and focus on a different question. When you come back to those answers, you'll have a better sense of what works best.

Momentum

I'm a big believer in doing the easy stuff first as it means progress can be made quickly and delivers a momentum that will help with the tougher tasks. This is especially important if you are planning to engage a team in the development of your Brand Arrow – you don't want to flummox the team by asking for a new vision for the brand before they have had their first coffee! The idea, as mentioned before, is that we are creating a pool of knowledge that will inform how we shape the brand, and as this is an iterative not linear process, we can choose the order that makes the most sense.

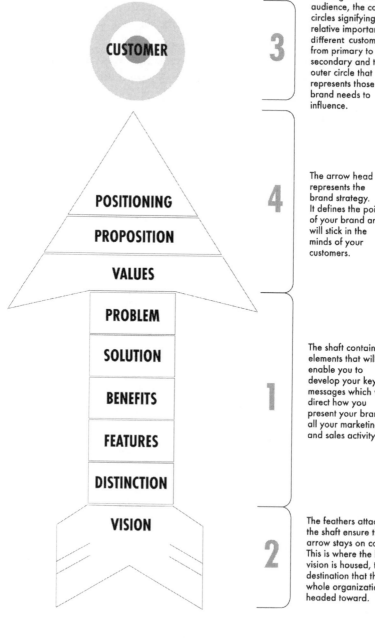

CUSTOMER

3 The target is the audience, the concentric circles signifying the relative importance of different customers – from primary to secondary and to the outer circle that represents those the brand needs to influence.

POSITIONING

PROPOSITION

VALUES

4 The arrow head represents the brand strategy. It defines the point of your brand and will stick in the minds of your customers.

PROBLEM

SOLUTION

BENEFITS

FEATURES

DISTINCTION

1 The shaft contains the elements that will enable you to develop your key messages which will direct how you present your brand in all your marketing and sales activity.

VISION

2 The feathers attached to the shaft ensure that the arrow stays on course. This is where the brand vision is housed, the destination that the whole organization is headed toward.

APPENDIX 2
Workshop Running Order

I'm suggesting that if you have done the hard yards and answered the Brand Arrow questions you will be able to build your Brand Arrow over the course of an eight-hour working day, or four sessions of two hours if you can't spare a whole day.

The order in which you complete the Brand Arrow is not the order the final brand strategy will be presented. The running order has been developed to allow you to make fast and easy progress in its development.

When I'm moderating a Brand Arrow workshop, I ask each participant to answer the first question on a Post-it note. Once done, we put them all up on the relevant section and, after discussion, agree a form of words that goes into the text box. We then take down the Post-its and go to the next question. When all the text boxes are filled up, the Brand Arrow is complete.

The following is broken down into four two-hour sessions:

Session 1: Key messaging (the shaft of the Brand Arrow)

1. Write a sentence that describes the most pressing need your customer has (BA9).

2. Write a sentence that describes how your brand meets that need (BA10).

3. List the three key benefits of your solution (BA19).

4. List the three key features of your solution (BA20).

5. Define what single thing makes your brand distinct from the competition (BA21, BA22).

6. Prioritize your five key sales and marketing messages (BA23).

This delivers both a deep dive into how you frame your services, and a prioritized list of your five key sales and marketing messages.

Session 2: Vision (the feathers at the base of the Brand Arrow)

1. Write up to a paragraph that captures the vision of the brand (BA1, BA2, BA5).

2. List the drivers and barriers to reaching that vision (BA6).

This will define the direction you are headed and the steps needed to ensure the brand can make progress toward it.

Session 3: Audience (the target the Brand Arrow is aimed at)

1. Summarize the brand's two or three key audiences (BA17).

2. List the five characteristics the key audiences all share (BA18).

This will provide a guide for identifying your addressable market as well ensuring the brand knows the overall characteristics of the audience.

Session 4: Brand strategy (the point of the Brand Arrow)

1. List the six characteristics or values of the brand (BA11, BA12).

2. In one or two words, define the brand positioning (BA7, BA8).

3. In around six words, express how the brand proposition would be expressed (BA24).

This brand strategy is competed last so that you can draw on the pool of knowledge created through the first three sessions.

Once completed, it's worth keeping the Brand Arrow up for a few days, and perhaps reconvening the team to review it before transferring the content of the text boxes onto a one-page Word document in the following order:

1. Vision

2. Brand strategy

3. Audience

4. Key messaging

BRAND ARROW QUESTIONS BY SESSION

Session 1: Key messaging (the shaft of the Brand Arrow)

Write a sentence that describes the most pressing need your customer has.

BA9: What is your customer's greatest need?

What is it you do for your customers? What is the problem that you are solving? This may seem like an easy question, but it isn't, because your customers may have lots of needs – or their needs may differ from one to the next. For this exercise, we need to define an overarching need because we are then going to focus on creating a brand that responds to that need. So, make a note of all of the needs using one sentence for each and then put them into an order with the most pressing need at the top of the list.

Write a sentence that describes how your brand meets that need.

BA10: How do you meet that need?

Now that you have defined your customer's most pressing need, describe how you are able to meet that need. Once you have done that, it will be useful to go down your list of needs and define your solutions for each one as this can be used later in the process. Remember though, it needs to be distinctive from others in the same sector and should stem from the work you have done in defining your positioning. Once you are done, you should have two sentences that capture the problem you are solving and how you plan to solve it. We will come back to these when we develop the brand messaging in chapter 10.

List the three key benefits of your solution.

BA19: Prioritize your five most important benefits.

To start with, go to the work you did for Brand Arrow question 6 in chapter 3 on your internal drivers, the things you are already really good at doing, and jot down those ones that relate to what you deliver to your customers. Now look at your services and add to the list the benefits they deliver to the customer – make sure you include tangible evidence that what you deliver does actually work! You'll end up with a list – try and keep that list to no more than five items. Now prioritize the list as directed in the chapter.

List the three key features of your solution.

BA20: Describe the features that enable the benefits to be delivered.

Think through or discuss with your team the features that enable each benefit to be delivered. Perhaps first of all note all the features and then put them into an order of the effectiveness – ideally you want to aim for around three per benefit. If you find you have one benefit that has five or six features it may be worth considering whether the single benefit could be split into two.

Define what single thing makes your brand distinct from the competition.

BA21: Define your competitors' brand strategies.

By auditing your competitors you will learn a great deal about them which will help enormously as you develop your own brand strategy. Start by making a list of the market leaders, those that have been in the sector the longest, the new entrants, brands that are not doing so well, and if not already captured, your direct competitors. You'll want to end up with a list of up to a dozen brands to review. This exercise will provide some great insights into what brand and marketing activity works and what doesn't, if there are any gaps in the provision of services that you could fill, and give you a good sense of what is already being done and what could be done better.

For each brand, open their website and you will most likely land on the homepage. In theory at least, this should contain the most important elements of the brand. It's a bit old fashioned to think of the homepage as a shop window but its role is to marshal the most valuable assets of the brand into a single place that will tell the customer why the brand is both relevant to them and different from others. Before scrolling down or clicking any of the links, look to see if there are any words under the logo, and what is the main headline and visual. If there is copy make a note of it along with how they structure their navigation (this is a great clue for where they see their priorities). Now draft what you think might be the brand proposition for each one.

BA22: Rank your competitor's marketing by quality and relevance to your brand.

Next, put yourself in the mindset of a prospective customer and spend time auditing each of your competitor's websites. Visit each page, be sure to review their most recent press releases and downloadable content and if you are feeling cheeky, subscribe to their newsletter. Capture their range of services, what kind of evidence they provide to substantiate their claims, and define the type of customer they are targeting. Note down their primary and secondary messaging and how the benefits and features of its product range are defined. I like to review all the brands in one go, usually on a large board divided into columns or a series of flip charts, as this will help you compare one to the other and provide a useful overview of the sector. Score out of 10 how well each one does in terms of brand and marketing activity, then score each one in terms of relevance to your own brand. This will provide you with a very useful way of seeing the type of brand and marketing that works in your sector, what to consider emulating and what to avoid.

Prioritize your five key sales and marketing messages.

BA23: Using the answers from previous Brand Arrow questions, put together a messaging hierarchy.

On the top of a flip chart, copy out the answers you gave to Brand Arrow questions 9 and 10 from chapter 5 (what is your customer's greatest need and how do you meet it?). Label the first sentence PROBLEM and the second sentence SOLUTION.

In slightly smaller text, note down the answers from Brand Arrow questions 19 and 20 from chapter 10 (prioritize your five most important benefits and describe the features that enable the benefits to be delivered). Label those two lists BENEFITS and FEATURES.

Now write out five sentences that start with a benefit and end with a solution. When you are done, go to chapters 4 and 11 and review what makes you different from your competitors (Brand Arrow questions 7 and 8, 21 and 22). Make sure your message hierarchy feels distinctly yours.

Finally, stand back, and with your right arm give your left-hand shoulder a pat – congratulations, you have just completed your message hierarchy!

Session 2: Vision (the feathers at the base of the Brand Arrow)

Write up to a paragraph that captures the vision of the brand.

BA1: Name the three key themes that characterize the sector you are in.

How would you capture the character of the sector, field, industry, etc. that you are in? Is it a sector that has gone through significant change in the last five years? If so, what has driven that change? A new entrant? Technology? Consumer behavior? Perhaps your sector hasn't changed at all and you are looking to shake things up? Or maybe a new brand has changed the dynamics of the sector? What kind of companies do you compete with? Are they all pretty much the same with only small differences separating them, or maybe there are fundamental differences in what each one offers. Aim to write three paragraphs, one for each theme.

BA2: What is the single most pressing need the sector is meeting and how might that change over time?

What do your customers want? What needs are you meeting? For example, getting legal expertise but without having to hire a lawyer, or the need to eat more healthily without it taking longer to source and prepare meals. Try and sum up the major need, or problem, the sector solves for its customers now. Once you are done, explore where the trends might be taking the sector and state what its needs might be in five and ten years.

BA5: Where do you want to get to in 10 years (think big!)?

It's a big question and not easy to answer. When I talk to clients about what their vision might be I always start off by asking about where they want to be in 12 months. This deals with important but transactional stuff like, hire a new person for the sales team or re-do the website – and allows us to focus on the bigger picture. I usually then go on to ask about what the future looks like in three to five years before settling on the big question of ten years plus. This releases us from important practical issues and almost gives us permission to be able to dream a little. At this point, I would say not to get worried about making it sound eloquent, or perfectly written. The framework we are working on together is iterative, so once you have a broad idea about where you are headed you can focus on the next part of the process. Once you have a better idea about what your brand strategy is, you can come back if needs be and rewrite the vision to better reflect your strategy.

List the drivers and barriers to reaching that vision.

BA6: What will help you get there? What will slow you down?

Consider what drivers you have to help you get to that vision and what barriers might there be to slow you down or even stop you reaching it. For drivers, consider what your key strengths are, for example, you may have a product that is superior to the competition, your team might be highly skilled or there is a need in the market that your product clearly meets. For barriers, note down the issues you feel need to be resolved, for example, lack of internal communications that means the team works in silos, a product that is failing behind its competitors or a website that does not promote the brand as well as it could. Try to bullet point five barriers and drivers with a supporting paragraph under each bullet.

Session 3: Audience (the target the Brand Arrow is aimed at)

Summarize the brand's two or three key audiences.

BA17: Categorize your top three target audiences.

List your top three target audiences based on their importance to your brand – you can rank them in terms of the revenue they bring to the brand or the market share they represent, for example. Under each, write a paragraph that provides a sense of who they are. You can use demographic data like age, gender and income; attitudinal information that captures their views on key market and societal subjects, and if it's a business customer you can define their role in the organization. What matters is that by the end of this you have a clear sense of the type of customers you are wanting to engage with.

List the five characteristics the key audiences all share.

BA18: What five characteristics do all your customers share?

We have talked about the role of the brand strategy as sitting above the component parts of an organization (different customers, products, markets, etc.) so that it can corral those differences into a cohesive whole. We now need to take the work done in segmenting the audiences and capture the common themes or threads that run through them all. I find an effective way of doing this is to write each audience type on a flip chart, put them next to each other, stand back, look to see the commonalities that characterize all your audiences, and make a note of the top five.

Session 4: Brand strategy (the point of the Brand Arrow)

List the six characteristics or values of the brand.

BA11: Define the values that sum up the character of your organization.

Spend some time exploring what things go really well in your organization, and try to capture the reasons you think they do. Have a look at your products and services and make a note of the values they embody. Very importantly, look also at what doesn't work so well and ask yourself what values you would need to adopt to deal with those issues. If it's just you, ask the people you deal with – customers and suppliers, for example. Look at your materials and ask yourself what values they are projecting. If there's more than one of you, ask the team; perhaps make it a confidential email or an anonymous suggestion box.

BA12: Choose six values and write a sentence that expresses exactly what you mean by each.

You will end up with a lot more than six values, and so look at clustering the responses into themes and then name the themes. For example, if there are a lot of responses around speed of delivery, fast response to customer queries, efficiencies in internal systems, you might cluster these round the word effectiveness. These will become your six values. Use the words in each cluster to write a sentence about each value to give a deeper sense of what that value stands for. This is important because it takes away any guesswork about the specific use of each value, it provides a very useful start for writing copy for marketing and sales, and it acknowledges that some values are a work in progress or even a response to an issue that has come up in the process.

In one or two words, define the brand positioning.

BA7: How would you describe the essence of your organization?

What are your truths? For Blue Yonder it was all about their approach to delivering decisions, for the IT company it was how they saw the world, and for Hampstead Tea it was about enrichment. Have a think, talk to your team and key customers, jot down some words that you feel reflect what lays at the heart of your organization. These words should focus on how you do things and not what those things are. With my own consulting work, I start by asking clients to sum up in a sentence the value of their brand. I then ask them to sum that up in a word or two. I'm always told that it's impossible, but I always get useful insights when those one or two words are expressed.

Once you have done that exercise, you should have around a dozen words. Put them down on a chart, stand back and ask yourself are these words true, do they resonate with your culture, are they distinctive, are they unique? Cross out the ones that don't make the grade and at the end of this you should have one or two words that have the potential to become your brand positioning.

BA8: Does the brand positioning mark you out as different from your key competitors?

> *"In around six words, express how the brand proposition would be expressed."*

Go back to the work you have done with your three key competitors in chapter 2 and consider what their positioning might be. How are they defining the problem and how are they solving it? This can be done quickly – usually the homepage of their website should provide you with all you need to get a sense of their point. How does it compare to yours? If you feel the words on your list of brand positionings are distinct and compelling, then we have a strong foundation to build from. If, however, you feel they are too close to your competitors, go back and explore how you can create a more distinctive brand positioning – better to do this now and not when you have just launched your new website!

In around six words, express how the brand proposition would be expressed.

BA24: Write a brand proposition based on the message hierarchy.

The end goal is to have a sentence that sums up the best, most compelling and relevant expression of your brand, what we referred to in chapter 5 as the brand proposition. With fresh flip chart paper, write down your brand positioning (Brand Arrow question 7 in chapter 4). Use the recently completed messaging hierarchy and your brand values (Brand Arrow questions 11 and 12) and take the first key message and see whether this could be used as a brand proposition – is it the right length (around six words), does it represent all the brand or just one feature, does it reflect the brand values.

Work through each key message and you will find either one of those lines works, or as is more likely, it will be a combination that will deliver the brand proposition. It's best to do this with a team as you can bounce ideas off one another. You'll see this task has been left to last so that all the exploration of the brand strategy has been completed.

ACKNOWLEDGEMENTS

Thanks to my "book club" who read through the book proposal and gave amazingly helpful and honest feedback, who have been with me through all the decisions on how to package up the content into something that looks like it's worth reading! In no particular order: Mark Tiderman, Christian Young, Sue Howard, Terry Stannard, Isne Villin, Mark Helvadjian, Jeremy Lindley, Mark Plummer, David Clamp and Tally Parr. Thanks also to the incredibly talented team that helped me design and promote the book – Sally Davidson, Richard Pagget and Adam Dickinson.

Thanks to Andrew Angus, Director of the full-time MBA at the Cranfield School of Management, who facilitated the engagement of Yali Edevbie and Kaushik Gupta – two brilliant MBA students – to act as my researchers for the book.

Thanks to Sales Supremo and good friend Tim Winfield who very patiently took me through the sales process that enabled me to write chapter 12, Everybody Needs to Sell. Thanks also to fellow brand strategist Patrick Gilmore who helped me solve a troublesome issue in the chapter on Brand Proposition.

Thanks to Robert McFarland who offered to share with me his own book proposal – to which I replied, 'What's a book proposal?!' This was hugely important for me as I was able to put some structure into my thinking and allow others to have something to respond to.

Thanks to my publishers Malcolm Down and Sarah Grace and their hugely talented team – vast amounts of knowledge, expertise and support were provided on a seemingly daily basis! Thanks also to three wonderful people in the publishing world who were so willing to give their time and wisdom to a complete novice – Jamie Marshall, Carlos Darby and Eloise Cook.

Finally, to my wonderful family, Liz, Adam, Matthew and Sophie. Thank you for the abundance of love, encouragement and practical advice on all things social media!

ENDORSEMENTS

"Bruce successfully equips marketers and business owners of all sizes with a powerful yet simple brand strategy framework – one which actually delivers results! A must read for all those who want to stand out from the crowd and drive real growth."

Mark Helvadjian, Founder, ShippingEasy.com and SCRUBD

"Magical! Bruce has integrated strategic planning, branding, marketing and storytelling into this compact, easy to read guide. Concepts that are often confusing and even contradictory are explained clearly and usefully. Invaluable!"

Jonathan Rosenthal. Co-Founder, Equal Exchange, US

"Anyone studying business should read this book. Bruce has created a useful structure to ensure that a business has a clear and succinct idea of its purpose and that everyone knows where they are headed."

Andrew Angus, Director of the full-time MBA, Cranfield School of Management

"Bruce is clear, succinct and relentlessly practical as he shares the positive difference a sharply focused brand can make to an organization. An inspiring and practical book, succinct and full of wisdom, that will help your organization focus and grow."

Jeremy Lindley, Board Director, Design Business Association

"What's Your Point? maps out a compelling and robust model for brand and marketing strategy, so marketing novices, start-ups and mature businesses needing a re-boot can create a route map for growth and success."

Stephen Woodford, CEO, Advertising Association

"If you are a start-up and want to understand why and how you should develop a brand strategy, then this book is for you."

Richard Anson, Strategy Director, True, Lecturer in Entrepreneurship at University College London

REFERENCES

Chapter 1

[1] Khan S.U. and Mufti O. "The Hot History and Cold Future of Brands". *Journal of Managerial Sciences*, Vol. 1, No. 1, 2007, p. 76 (Accessed 17 July 2019)

[2] Commercial Advertisement. Department Washington. Available at: https://depts.washington.edu/chinaciv/graph/tcommain.htm (Accessed: 16 July 2019)

[3] Campbell-Dollaghan, K. "The Strange Medieval Origins of Modern Logos". Gizmodo. 2014. Available at: https://gizmodo.com/the-strange-medieval-origins-of-modern-logos-1670331631 (Accessed: 16 July 2019)

[4] Cooksongold. "A Brief History of Jewellery Hallmarking". The Bench. 2016. Available at: https://www.cooksongold.com/blog/jewellery-tips/a-brief-history-of-hallmarking (Accessed: 16 July 2019)

[5] "What To Do When There Are Too Many Product Choices On The Store Shelves". Consumer Reports. 2014. Available at: https://www.consumerreports.org/cro/magazine/2014/03/too-many-product-choices-in-supermarkets/index.htm (Accessed: 9 July 2019)

[6] "How Many Products Does Amazon Actually Carry? And in What Categories?" Business Wire. 2016. Available at: https://www.businesswire.com/news/home/20160614006063/en/Products-Amazon-Carry-Categories (Accessed: 9 July 2019)

[7] Orange history: History highlights. Orange. Available at: https://www.orange.com/sirius/histoire/en/history-highlights (Accessed: 9 July 2019)

[8] "Superbrands case studies: Orange". campaign. 2002. Available at: https://www.campaignlive.co.uk/article/superbrands-case-studies-orange/164341 (Accessed: 9 July 2019)

[9] "Orange in the world". Orange. Available at: https://www.orange.com/en/Group/Orange-in-the-world (Accessed: 9 July 2019)

[10] "Sky Mobile to allow customers to keep unused data". Belfast Telegraph Digital. 2017. Available at: https://www.belfasttelegraph.co.uk/business/news/sky-mobile-to-allow-customers-to-keep-unused-data-35343073.html (Accessed: 9 July 2019)

Chapter 2

[11] Jane. "Facts about shipping containers". Billie Box. 2012. Available at: https://www.billiebox.co.uk/facts-about-shipping-containers (Accessed: 9 July 2019)

[12] "ISO Containers Information". Engineering 360. Available at: https://www.globalspec.com/learnmore/material_handling_packaging_equipment/material_handling_equipment/iso_containers (Accessed: 9 July 2019)

[13] "All about us". ISO. Available at: https://www.iso.org/about-us.html (Accessed: 9 July 2019)

[14] "ISO 10668:2010 - Brand valuation — Requirements for monetary brand valuation". ISO. Available at: https://www.iso.org/standard/46032.html (Accessed: 9 July 2019)

[15] "ISO 10668:2010 - Brand valuation — Requirements for monetary brand valuation". ISO. Available at: https://www.iso.org/standard/46032.html (Accessed: 9 July 2019)

[16] Badenhausen K. "The World's Most Valuable Brands 2018". Forbes. 2018. Available at: https://www.forbes.com/sites/kurtbadenhausen/2018/05/23/the-worlds-most-valuable-brands-2018/#4c59f8b3610c (Accessed: 9 July 2019)

[17] "Overview of ISO 10668: Brand Valuation, Requirements for Monetary Brand Valuation, 10 August 2011". Australian Marketing Institute. Available at: https://brandfinance.com/images/upload/iso_10668_overview.pdf (Accessed: 17 July 2019)

[18] "Global mobile consumer survey: US edition". Available at: https://www2.deloitte.com/us/en/pages/technology-media-and-telecommunications/articles/global-mobile-consumer-survey-us-edition.html (Accessed: 29 July 2019)

[19] "ISO/IEC 17025:2017(en). General requirements for the competence of testing and calibration laboratories". ISO. Available at: https://www.iso.org/obp/ui/#iso:std:iso-iec:17025:ed-3:v1:en (Accessed: 9 July 2019)

[20] Murray A. "Should I spend £1.45 on branded painkillers, or 19p at the supermarket?" *The Telegraph*. 2015. Available at: https://www.telegraph.co.uk/finance/personalfinance/money-saving-tips/11956383/Should-I-spend-1.45-on-branded-painkillers-or-19p-at-the-supermarket.html (Accessed: 9 July 2019)

[21] Ahsan S. "Do branded painkillers work better than cheaper generic ones?" *The Guardian*. 2016. Available at: https://www.theguardian.com/science/2016/oct/03/do-branded-painkillers-work-better-than-cheaper-generic-ones-iboprofen-nurofen (Accessed: 9 July 2019)

[22]Simpson J. " Finding Brand Success In The Digital World". Forbes. 2017. Available at: https://www.forbes.com/sites/forbesagencycouncil/2017/08/25/finding-brand-success-in-the-digital-world/#675830ca626e (Accessed: 9 July 2019)

[23]O'Reilly L. "Apple mysteriosuly stopped disclosing how much it spends on ads". Business Insider. 2016. Available at: https://www.businessinsider.com/apple-stopped-disclosing-ad-spend-2016-11?r=US&IR=T (Accessed: 9 July 2019)

[24]"CAI". idealist. Available at: https://www.idealist.org/en/nonprofit/931ea82078 b1438b892405b3fe5e79ea-cai-new-york (Accessed: 9 July 2019)

Chapter 3

[25]Long T. "May 25, 1961: JFK Vows to Put American on Moon by Decade's End". Wired. 2012. Available at: https://www.wired.com/2012/05/may-25-1961-jfk-vows-to-put-american-on-moon-by-decades-end (Accessed: 10 July 2019)

[26]Jansen T. "JFK and the Janitor: the importance of understanding the WHY that is behind what we do". beqom. 2014. Available at: https://www.beqom.com/blog/jfk-and-the-janitor (Accessed: 10 July 2019)

Chapter 4

[27]Elliott A. "Honouring the biggest ship ever built, and Hong Kong's role in getting her afloat". Post Magazine. 2018. Available at: https://www.scmp.com/magazines/post-magazine/long-reads/article/2135801/honouring-biggest-ship-ever-built-and-hong-kongs (Accessed: 13 July 2019)

[28]Elliott A. "Bombed and resurrected: Fascinating story of the largest ship ever built, which was twice the size of the Titanic and was SUNK but was dragged up to sail again". Mail Online. 2017. Available at: https://www.dailymail.co.uk/travel/travel_news/article-4779070/History-Seawise-Giant-world-s-largest-ship.html (Accessed: 13 July 2019)

[29]Armstrong S. "Saatchi brothers mark 40 years since the foundation of their ad agency". The Guardian. 2010. Available at: https://www.theguardian.com/media/2010/sep/06/saatchi-brothers-40-years-advertising (Accessed: 13 July 2019)

Chapter 5

[30]Watson N. "Film Review: Manhattan, 'Woody Allen's love letter to the city'". Plymouth Arts Cinema. 2017. Available at: https://plymouthartscentre.org/film-review-manhattan-woody-allens-love-letter-city (Accessed: 13 July 2019)

[31]"Do You Know GE?". GE. Available at: https://www.ge.com/brand (Accessed: 17 July 2019)

[32]"About Us". slack. Available at: https://slack.com/intl/en-gb/about (Accessed: 13 July 2019)

[33]"About the newspaper". *Financial Times*. Available at: https://web.archive.org/web/20120108062240/http://help.ft.com/newspaper-delivery/about-the-newspaper/#axzz3ZDPTGgyZ (Accessed: 17 July 2019)

[34]Billings C. "'No FT no comment' and 'Let your fingers do the walking' join slogan hall of fame". campaign. 2002. Available at: https://www.campaignlive.co.uk/article/no-ft-no-comment-let-fingers-walking-join-slogan-hall-fame/140633 (Accessed: 13 July 2019)

Chapter 6

[35]Clarke L. "IKEA: Corporate Culture of the Heart". 6Q Blog. Available at: https://inside.6q.io/ikea-corporate-culture-of-the-heart (Accessed: 14 April 2019)

[36]List of countries with IKEA stores. Available at: https://en.m.wikipedia.org/wiki/List_of_countries_with_IKEA_stores (Accessed 29 July 2019)

[37]Bhattarai A. "Ikea has changed the way we think about furniture". *The Washington Post*. 2018. Available at: https://www.washingtonpost.com/news/business/wp/2018/01/28/ikea-has-changed-the-way-we-think-about-furniture/?utm_term=.9b45174380cf (Accessed: 8 July 2019)

[38]"Gillis Lundgren". *The Sunday Times*. 2016. Available at: https://www.thetimes.co.uk/article/gillis-lundgren-j0xtwg80l (Accessed: 5 July 2019)

[39]"Ikea is a more than just somewhere to buy convenient flatpack furniture - it's a design goldmine". *The* Telegraph. 2018. Available at: https://www.telegraph.co.uk/property/interiors/ikea-just-somewhere-buy-convenient-flatpack-furniture-design (Accessed 17 July 2019)

[40]"Our values make us different". Sainsbury's Strategic Report. Available at: https://www.about.sainsburys.co.uk/~/media/Files/S/Sainsburys/pdf-downloads/sainsburys-ar-2017-values (Accessed: 16 April 2019)

[41]"Virgin branded companies". Virgin. Available at: https://www.virgin.com/virgin group/company/branded (Accessed: 5 July 2019)

[42]"Our purpose and values". Virgin. Available at: https://www.virgin.com/virgin-management-limited/careers/OurPurposeandValues (Accessed: 14 April 2019)

[43]Rob. "Relax in an Upper Class seat in your nearest Virgin Money lounge!" Head for Points. 2014. Available at: https://www.headforpoints.com/2014/03/28/relax-in-a-virgin-upper-class-seat-in-your-nearest-virgin-money-lounge (Accessed: 23 April 2019)

[44]Saran C. "Virgin Holidays simplifies holiday experiences with Adobe". ComputerWeekly.com. 2017. Available at: https://www.computerweekly.com/news/450430191/Virgin-Holidays-simplifies-holiday-experiences-with-Adobe (Accessed: 22 April 2019)

[45]"Virgin Trains gives its customers a voice with Amazon Alexa ticketing partnership". SmartRail World. 2018. Available at: https://www.smartrailworld.com/virgin-trains-amazon-alexa-ticketing-partnership (Accessed: 16 April 2019)

[46]"Timeline: How Virgin has changed the world". Virgin. Available at: https://www.virgin.com/disruptors/timeline-how-virgin-has-changed-world (Accessed: 17 July 2019)

[47]Stahler P. "We 'totally screwed up': Values and Behaviors in Volkswagen business model. Business Model Innovation. 2015. Available at: http://blog.business-model-innovation.com/2015/09/values-and-behaviors-in-volkswagen-business-model (Accessed: 14 April 2019)

[48]Thompson N. "Health Care Is Broken. Oscar Health Thinks Tech Can Fix It". Wired. 2018. Available at: https://www.wired.com/story/oscar-health-ceo-mario-schlosser-interview (Accessed: 16 April 2019)

[49]Thompson N. "Health Care Is Broken. Oscar Health Thinks Tech Can Fix It". Wired. 2018. Available at: https://www.wired.com/story/oscar-health-ceo-mario-schlosser-interview/ (Accessed: 16 April 2019)

[50] Blake I. "Do YOU eat this much? Average British shopper enjoys 187 chocolate bars every YEAR". Mail Online. 2017. Available at: https://www.dailymail.co.uk/femail/food/article-5549105/Mintel-reports-average-British-person-ate-chocolate-Europe-2017.html (Accessed: 16 July 2019)

[51] "Our Story". Hotel Chocolat. Available at: https://www.hotelchocolat.com/uk/engaged-ethics/our-people/Our-Story.html (Accessed: 14 April 2019)

[52] "Our Story". Hotel Chocolat. Available at: https://www.hotelchocolat.com/uk/engaged-ethics/our-people/Our-Story.html (Accessed: 14 April 2019)

[53] "Our Story". Hotel Chocolat. Available at: https://www.hotelchocolat.com/uk/engaged-ethics/our-people/Our-Story.html (Accessed: 14 April 2019)

Chapter 7

[54] Protz R. "Arts that others don't reach...". *The Guardian*. 2001. Available at: https://www.theguardian.com/travel/2001/feb/11/copenhagen.denmark.travelfoodanddrink (Accessed: 13 July 2019)

[55] "Carlsberg pours its heart out with Pilsner relaunch, admits it 'Probably' wasn't the best". The Drum, Available at: https://www.thedrum.com/news/2019/04/15/carlsberg-pours-its-heart-out-with-pilsner-relaunch-admits-it-probably-wasnt-the (Accessed 18 July 2019)

[56] Redd W. "Where Did The Google Name Come From?" 2018. Available at: https://allthatsinteresting.com/google-name (Accessed: 16 July 2019)

[57] McAlone N. "The true story behind Google's first name: BackRub". Business Insider. 2015. Available at: https://www.businessinsider.com/the-true-story-behind-googles-first-name-backrub-2015-10?r=US&IR=T (Accessed: 16 July 2019)

[58] Definition of "google" in English. Lexico. Available at: https://www.lexico.com/en/definition/google (Accessed: 16 July 2019)

[59] "Parker Harris on co-founding Salesforce.com". Salesforce. Available at: https://admin.salesforce.com/parker-harris-co-founding-salesforce-com (Accessed: 18 July 2019)

[60] "About Us". PayPal. Available at: https://www.paypal.com/uk/webapps/mpp/about (Accessed: 16 July 2019)

[61] Myers D. "25 Things You Didn't Know About Coca-Cola". The Daily Meal. 2019. Available at: https://www.thedailymeal.com/eat/things-you-didnt-know-about-coca-cola-gallery (Accessed: 16 July 2019)

[62] McCreary M. "How a 17-Year-Old With $1,000 Started Subway and Became a Billionaire". Entrepreneur Europe. 2018. Available at: https://www.entrepreneur.com/article/313130 (Accessed: 16 July 2019)

[63] Teather D. "O2 breathes life into Cellnet". *The Guardian*. 2001. Available at: https://www.theguardian.com/business/2001/sep/04/11 (Accessed: 16 July 2019)

[64] McCormick R. "Britain's second-largest carrier O2 to be bought out in $15 billion deal". The Verge. 2015. Available at: https://www.theverge.com/2015/1/22/7875025/british-carrier-o2-15-billion-deal (Accessed: 16 July 2019)

[65] McIlroy AJ. "Post Office tries a change of name after 350 years". *The Telegraph*. 2001. Available at: https://www.telegraph.co.uk/news/uknews/1314134/Post-Office-tries-a-change-of-name-after-350-years.html (Accessed: 16 July 2019)

[66] McIlroy AJ. "Post Office tries a change of name after 350 years". *The Telegraph*. 2001. Available at: https://www.telegraph.co.uk/news/uknews/1314134/Post-Office-tries-a-change-of-name-after-350-years.html (Accessed: 16 July 2019)

[67] Fagan M. "Consignia name lost in post as Royal Mail returns". *The Telegraph*. 2002. Available at: https://www.telegraph.co.uk/finance/2764832/Consignia-name-lost-in-post-as-Royal-Mail-returns.html (Accessed: 16 July 2019)

[68] Rivkin S. "How Did Apple Computer Get Its Brand Name?" Branding Strategy Insider. 2011. Available at: https://www.brandingstrategyinsider.com/2011/11/how-did-apple-computer-get-its-brand-name.html#.XS2w61B7nBl (Accessed: 16 July 2019)

Chapter 8

[69] Quote by Napoleon Bonaparte: *"Un bon croquis vaut mieux qu'un long discours..."*. Goodreads. Available at: https://www.goodreads.com/quotes/135658-un-bon-croquis-vaut-mieux-qu-un-long-discours-a-good (Accessed: 16 July 2019)

[70] "Most Valuable Apparel Brand? Nike Just Does It Again". Brand Finance. 2019. Available at: https://brandfinance.com/news/press-releases/most-valuable-apparel-brand-nike-just-does-it-again (Accessed: 16 July 2019)

[71] Natividad A. "Stella Artois Becomes Isabella Artois, Honoring Its First CEO … From 300 Years Ago". Muse by Clio. 2019. Available at: https://musebycl.io/advertising/stella-artois-becomes-isabella-artois-honoring-its-first-ceo-300-years-ago (Accessed: 16 July 2019)

[72] Frohlich TC, Sauter MB. "The oldest corporate logos in the world". msn lifestyle. 2019. Available at: https://www.msn.com/en-za/lifestyle/lifestyle-news-feature/the-oldest-corporate-logos-in-the-world/ar-BBVDKP2 (Accessed: 16 July 2019)

[73] Baker C. "Behind the Red Triangle: The Bass Pale Ale Brand and Logo". Logoworks Blog. 2013. Available at: https://www.logoworks.com/blog/bass-pale-ale-brand-and-logo (Accessed: 16 July 2019)

[74] Greenbaum H. "Who Made That Campbell's Soup Label?" *The New York Times*. 2011. Available at: https://6thfloor.blogs.nytimes.com/2011/05/09/who-made-that-campbells-soup-label (Accessed: 16 July 2019)

[75] Boeriu H. "The History of the MINI Cooper". BMW Blog. 2012. Available at: https://www.bmwblog.com/2012/07/05/the-history-of-the-mini-cooper (Accessed: 16 July 2019)

[76] Thorpe L. "Here's Everything You Need to Know About Levi's' Two Horse, Red Tab, and Batwing Logos". Highsnobelity. 2018. Available at: https://www.highsnobiety.com/p/levis-logo-history (Accessed: 16 July 2019)

[77] Kate. "How Much Does a Logo Cost in 2018?" Logojoy. 2018. Available at: https://logojoy.com/blog/how-much-does-a-logo-cost (Accessed: 2 May 2019)

[78] "10 fashion lessons from Giorgio Armani". Bright Side. Available at: https://bright-side.me/article/10-fashion-lessons-from-giorgio-armani-62855 (Accessed: 16 July 2019)

[79] Peate S. "Show your colours: The psychology of colour and design in branding". Fabrik. 2017. Available at: https://fabrikbrands.com/the-psychology-of-colour-and-design (Accessed: 18 July 2019)

[80] "Best Global Brands 2018". Interbrand. 2018. Available at: https://www.interbrand.com/best-brands/best-global-brands/2018 (Accessed: 18 July 2019)

Chapter 9

[81]"John Lydgate". Encyclopedia.com. Available at: https://www.encyclopedia.com/people/literature-and-arts/english-literature-1499-biographies/john-lydgate (Accessed: 16 July 2019)

[82]"John Lydgate quotes". AZ Quotes. Available at: https://www.azquotes.com/author/42820-John_Lydgate (Accessed: 16 July 2019)

[83]Quote by John Lydgate: "You can please some of the people all of the time...". goodreads. Available at: https://www.goodreads.com/quotes/699462-you-can-please-some-of-the-people-all-of-the (Accessed: 16 July 2019)

[84]"What is Organizational Culture? Definition and Examples". Market Business News. Available at: https://marketbusinessnews.com/financial-glossary/organizational-culture-definition-examples (Accessed: 16 July 2019)

[85]Kukreja S. "Edgar Schein's Model of Organizational Culture". Management Study HQ. Available at: https://www.managementstudyhq.com/edgar-schein-model-theory.html (Accessed: 16 July 2019)

[86]Kukreja S. "Edgar Schein's Model of Organizational Culture". Management Study HQ. Available at: https://www.managementstudyhq.com/edgar-schein-model-theory.html (Accessed: 16 July 2019)

[87]Definition of "demography". Online Etymology Dictionary. Available at: https://www.etymonline.com/word/demography (Accessed: 16 July 2019)

[88]Mancall-Bitel N. "Everywhere Around the World Where McDonald's Serves Beer". supercall. 2017. Available at: https://www.supercall.com/culture/mcdonalds-beer (Accessed: 16 July 2019)

Chapter 10

[89]*Monty Python and the Holy Grail*. Netflix. Available at: https://www.netflix.com/gb/title/771476 (Accessed: 16 July 2019)

[90]"Trojan War". History. Available at: https://www.history.com/topics/ancient-history/trojan-war (Accessed: 18 July 2019)

[91]Woods J. "The evolution of the data center: Timeline from the Mainframe to the Cloud". Silicon Angle. Available at: https://siliconangle.com/2014/03/05/the-evolution-of-the-data-center-timeline-from-the-mainframe-to-the-cloud-tc0114 (Accessed: 18 July 2018)

Chapter 11

[92] Daily E. "How Michael Jordan's Nike Deal Changed Sports Marketing Forever". Edgar Daily. 2018. Available at: https://edgardaily.com/articles/how-michael-jordans-nike-deal-changed-sports-marketing-forever (Accessed: 2 May 2019)

[93] Lin X. "The Brand Equity of Nike, what makes it the best sports brand ever?" Medium. 2017. Available at: https://medium.com/@xlin6/the-brand-equity-of-nike-what-makes-it-the-best-sports-brand-ever-561a24fd296e (Accessed: 2 May 2019)

[94] Daily E. "How Michael Jordan's Nike Deal Changed Sports Marketing Forever". Edgar Daily. 2018. Available at: https://edgardaily.com/articles/how-michael-jordans-nike-deal-changed-sports-marketing-forever (Accessed: 2 May 2019)

[95] Lodge M. "Why Nike's Jordan Brand Isn't Flying as High These Days". The Street. 2018. Available at: https://www.thestreet.com/investing/why-nike-s-jordan-brand-isn-t-flying-as-high-these-days-14637954 (Accessed: 16 July 2019)

[96] Levinson P. "How Nike almost ended up with a very different name". Business Insider. 2016. Available at: https://www.businessinsider.com/how-nike-got-its-name-2016-1?r=US&IR=T (Accessed: 18 July 2019)

[97] Smithers, R. "Global Fairtrade sales reach £4.4bn following 15% growth during 2013". *The Guardian*. 2014. Available at: https://www.theguardian.com/global-development/2014/sep/03/global-fair-trade-sales-reach-4-billion-following-15-per-cent-growth-2013 (Accessed: 18 July 2019)

[98] Davies I., Doherty, B. and Knox, C. "The Rise and Stall of a Fair Trade Pioneer: The Cafédirect Story". *Journal of Business Ethics*, Vol. 92, No. 1, 2010, pp. 127–147

[99] Davies I., Doherty, B. and Knox, C. "The Rise and Stall of a Fair Trade Pioneer: The Cafédirect Story". *Journal of Business Ethics*, Vol. 92, No. 1, 2010, pp. 127–147

[100] Cafédirect plc. Report and financial statements for the year ended 31 December 2017. Available at: https://www.cafedirect.co.uk/wp-content/uploads/2018/06/Cafedirect-plc-Draft-Stats-ye-31-Dec-2017-FINAL-with-sigs.pdf (Accessed 18 July 2019)

Chapter 12

[101] Kenton W. "Elevator Pitch". Investopedia. 2017. Available at: https://www.

REFERENCES

investopedia.com/terms/e/elevatorpitch.asp (Accessed: 16 July 2019)

[102] Ainsworth R. "Attention spans are getting shorter. Or are they?" Source Global Research. Available at: https://www.sourceglobalresearch.com/attention-spans-are-getting-shorter-or-are-they (Accessed: 16 July 2019)

NOTES